HEALTH CARE IN TRANSITION

MEDICARE PART D PRESCRIPTION DRUG BENEFIT

ELEMENTS, PROVISIONS AND INTEGRITY ISSUES

HEALTH CARE IN TRANSITION

Additional books in this series can be found on Nova's website under the Series tab.

Additional e-books in this series can be found on Nova's website under the e-book tab.

HEALTH CARE IN TRANSITION

MEDICARE PART D PRESCRIPTION DRUG BENEFIT

ELEMENTS, PROVISIONS AND INTEGRITY ISSUES

ELENA MARSHALL
EDITOR

nova publishers
New York

Library of Congress Cataloging-in-Publication Data

ISBN: 978-1-63482-524-5

Published by Nova Science Publishers, Inc. † New York

CONTENTS

PREFACE

This book discusses the prescription drug benefit of Medicare Part D. It also examines practices for promoting prescription drug program integrity, and the extent that CMS's oversight of Medicare Part D program integrity, including the program integrity contractors, reflects these practices.

Chapter 1 – The Medicare Prescription Drug, Improvement, and Modernization Act of 2003 (MMA, P.L. 108-173) established a voluntary, outpatient prescription drug benefit under Medicare Part D, effective January 1, 2006. Medicare Part D provides coverage through private prescription drug plans (PDPs) that offer only drug coverage, or through Medicare Advantage (MA) prescription drug plans (MA-PDs) that offer coverage as part of broader, managed care plans. Private drug plans participating in Part D bear some financial risk, though federal subsidies cover most program costs in an effort to encourage participation and keep benefits affordable.

At a minimum, Medicare drug plans must offer a "standard coverage" package of benefits or alternative coverage that is actuarially equivalent to a standard plan. Plans may also offer enhanced benefits. While all plans must meet certain minimum requirements, there can be significant differences among offerings in terms of benefit design, specific drugs included in formularies (i.e., list of covered drugs), cost-sharing for particular drugs, or the level of monthly premiums. In general, beneficiaries can enroll in a plan, or change plan enrollment, when they first become eligible for Medicare or during open enrollment periods each November-December. For plan year 2014, there are from 28 to 39 PDPs in each of the nation's 34 PDP regions, as well as Medicare Advantage and additional low-income plans. Because sponsors are allowed to change plan offerings from year to year, beneficiaries must carefully review their annual choices to select the plans that best meet their needs.

A key element of the Part D program is enhanced coverage for low-income individuals. Persons with incomes up to 150% of the federal poverty level and assets below set limits are eligible for extra assistance with Medicare Part D premiums and cost-sharing. Individuals enrolled in both Medicare and Medicaid (so-called dual-eligibles), and certain other low-income beneficiaries, are automatically enrolled in no-premium plans, which are Part D plans that have premiums at, or below, specified levels. In recent years, the number of no-premium plans available to low-income subsidy recipients has been declining.

In 2012, about 31.9 million Medicare beneficiaries received prescription drug benefits through a PDP or a MA-PD; with about a third receiving a low-income subsidy. Another 5.6 million received drug assistance through a Part D-subsidized retiree health plan, while 5.7 million Medicare beneficiaries had separate, private drug coverage. Overall, about 63% of Medicare beneficiaries had drug coverage through Part D plans, and 85% had some type of drug coverage, either PDP or MP-PD plans, retiree coverage or private insurance of comparable scope. Part D expenditures were estimated to be about $70 billion in calendar year 2013.

Medicare Part D has cost less than forecast since its inception, due in part to lower-than-predicted enrollment and high use of less expensive generic drugs.

Chapter 2 – Recent media reports and law enforcement actions have highlighted the problem of prescription drug fraud, waste, and abuse in the United States. Medicare, and the Part D prescription drug benefit, are susceptible to such fraud—a risk made greater by Medicare's size, scope, and complexity. GAO and others have raised questions about CMS's oversight of its activities to address fraud, waste, and abuse in Part D, as well as oversight of the contractors tasked with this work.

GAO examined (1) practices for promoting prescription drug program integrity, and (2) the extent that CMS's oversight of Medicare Part D program integrity, including the program integrity contractors, reflects these practices. To develop a list of practices, GAO interviewed 14 stakeholder groups involved in various aspects of prescription drug program integrity, including provider, beneficiary, and anti-fraud groups; identified and reviewed related documents; and conducted a search of eight bibliographic databases that included peer-reviewed articles and government documents. GAO organized the practices based on the three categories of GAO's Fraud

Prevention Framework. To determine how CMS's oversight reflects these practices, GAO analyzed agency documents, such as contracts, manuals, work products, and CMS audits of contractors; and interviewed agency officials.

Chapter 1

MEDICARE PART D PRESCRIPTION DRUG BENEFIT*

Suzanne M. Kirchhoff and Patricia A. Davis

SUMMARY

The Medicare Prescription Drug, Improvement, and Modernization Act of 2003 (MMA, P.L. 108-173) established a voluntary, outpatient prescription drug benefit under Medicare Part D, effective January 1, 2006. Medicare Part D provides coverage through private prescription drug plans (PDPs) that offer only drug coverage, or through Medicare Advantage (MA) prescription drug plans (MA-PDs) that offer coverage as part of broader, managed care plans. Private drug plans participating in Part D bear some financial risk, though federal subsidies cover most program costs in an effort to encourage participation and keep benefits affordable.

At a minimum, Medicare drug plans must offer a "standard coverage" package of benefits or alternative coverage that is actuarially equivalent to a standard plan. Plans may also offer enhanced benefits. While all plans must meet certain minimum requirements, there can be significant differences among offerings in terms of benefit design, specific drugs included in formularies (i.e., list of covered drugs), cost-sharing for particular drugs, or the level of monthly premiums. In general, beneficiaries can enroll in a plan, or change plan enrollment, when they

* This is an edited, reformatted and augmented version of a Congressional Research Service publication, No. R40611, dated October 8, 2014.

first become eligible for Medicare or during open enrollment periods each November-December. For plan year 2014, there are from 28 to 39 PDPs in each of the nation's 34 PDP regions, as well as Medicare Advantage and additional low-income plans. Because sponsors are allowed to change plan offerings from year to year, beneficiaries must carefully review their annual choices to select the plans that best meet their needs.

A key element of the Part D program is enhanced coverage for low-income individuals. Persons with incomes up to 150% of the federal poverty level and assets below set limits are eligible for extra assistance with Medicare Part D premiums and cost-sharing. Individuals enrolled in both Medicare and Medicaid (so-called dual-eligibles), and certain other low-income beneficiaries, are automatically enrolled in no-premium plans, which are Part D plans that have premiums at, or below, specified levels. In recent years, the number of no-premium plans available to low-income subsidy recipients has been declining.

In 2012, about 31.9 million Medicare beneficiaries received prescription drug benefits through a PDP or a MA-PD; with about a third receiving a low-income subsidy. Another 5.6 million received drug assistance through a Part D-subsidized retiree health plan, while 5.7 million Medicare beneficiaries had separate, private drug coverage. Overall, about 63% of Medicare beneficiaries had drug coverage through Part D plans, and 85% had some type of drug coverage, either PDP or MP-PD plans, retiree coverage or private insurance of comparable scope. Part D expenditures were estimated to be about $70 billion in calendar year 2013.

Medicare Part D has cost less than forecast since its inception, due in part to lower-than-predicted enrollment and high use of less expensive generic drugs.

OVERVIEW

On January 1, 2014, the Medicare prescription drug program (Medicare Part D) began its ninth year of operation. Congress created Part D in the Medicare Prescription Drug, Improvement, and Modernization Act of 2003 (MMA, P.L. 108-173), effective January 1, 2006. The MMA provides a voluntary, outpatient prescription drug benefit for Medicare beneficiaries. The law also made Part D the primary source of drug coverage for individuals covered under both Medicare and Medicaid, (so-called dual-eligibles). Part D has been modified by a series of statutes since 2003, most recently by the Patient Protection and Affordable Care Act of 2010 as amended (ACA, P.L. 111-148; P.L. 111-152).[1]

Part D coverage is provided through private insurance plans (PDPs) that offer only drug coverage, or through Medicare Advantage (MA) plans (MA-PDs) that offer drug coverage as part of a broader, Medicare Part C managed care benefit. Alternatively, beneficiaries may be enrolled in retiree prescription drug plans offered by their former employers. The MMA provides subsidies for retiree drug plans as an incentive to employers to continue such plans. (See "Retiree Drug Subsidy.")

About 37.9 million Medicare beneficiaries were enrolled in Part D plans in September 2014. Of that total, about 23.4 million were in PDPs and about 14 million were in MA-PDs.[2] A major focus of the Part D program is providing subsidized coverage to qualified, low-income beneficiaries. Individuals with incomes up to 150% of the federal poverty level and limited assets are eligible for a low-income subsidy (LIS). The LIS reduces beneficiaries' out-of-pocket spending by paying for all, or some, of the Part D monthly premium and annual deductible, and limiting co-payments or co-insurance. The LIS is progressive, meaning the lowest-income beneficiaries receive the greatest assistance. In 2013, about 11.5 million beneficiaries received the LIS.[3]

The ACA made major changes to Part D in an effort to improve coverage and to make the premium structure more progressive by requiring higher-income beneficiaries to pay more for coverage. Starting in 2011, the ACA required Part D enrollees with incomes above a certain threshold to pay a monthly surcharge in addition to their regular plan premiums. (See "Premium Surcharges for High Income Enrollees.") In addition, the ACA phases out the "doughnut hole" by requiring drug manufacturers to provide a 50% discount for brand-name drugs purchased by beneficiaries in the Part D coverage gap, or "doughnut hole"[4] and gradually phases in Medicare subsidies to cover 75% of the cost of generic drugs and 25% of the cost of brand name drugs in the coverage gap. (See "The Coverage Gap.")

Medicare Part D relies on participating private insurance plans to provide coverage and bear part of the financial risk of the program. All Part D plans must meet certain minimum requirements, though there are significant variations among plans in terms of benefit design including differences in premiums, drug formularies (i.e., lists of covered drugs), and cost-sharing for particular drugs. In 2014, there are 1,169 stand-alone PDPs and 1,615 MA-PDs, nationwide.[5]

ELIGIBILITY

In general, anyone who is entitled to Medicare Part A and/or enrolled in Part B is eligible to enroll in a Medicare Part D drug plan. In addition, an individual must permanently reside within one of the 34 designated PDP regions in the United States; anyone who is living abroad or is incarcerated is not eligible.[6]

For most people, joining Part D is voluntary, although dual-eligible beneficiaries (See "Full-Subsidy-Eligible Individuals") are automatically enrolled. Medicare beneficiaries cannot be turned down for Part D coverage due to pre-existing health conditions or high utilization of prescription drugs.

The most recent, comprehensive Part D data from CMS, for plan year 2012, show that of the more than 50.8 million Medicare beneficiaries, 31.9 million were enrolled in either a stand-alone Part D prescription drug plan (19.9 million) or in a MA-PD plan (12 million). An additional 5.6 million had prescription drug coverage through a former employer that received a Part D subsidy for a portion of their coverage. About 5.7 million Medicare beneficiaries had drug coverage through another source, such as the Federal Employees Health Benefits program, TRICARE or private coverage. Approximately 7.7 million beneficiaries (about 15%) did not have drug coverage equivalent to Part D. (See **Table 1**.)

Table 1.Total Medicare Beneficiaries with Prescription Drug Coverage, 2012 (in millions)

Description	2012	Percent of Eligible
Medicare Beneficiaries Eligible for Part D	50.8	100%
Medicare Part D	31.9	63%
Stand-Alone PDP	19.9	39%
MA with Drug Coverage	12.0	24%
Medicare Retiree Drug Subsidy (RDS)	5.6	11%
Other Creditable Drug Coverage	5.7	11%
Total Beneficiaries with Drug Coverage	43.2	85%
Beneficiaries with No Coverage	7.7	15%

Source: *Medicare and Medicaid Statistical Supplement*, 2013 Edition, Tables 14.1 and 14.8, http://www.cms.gov/Research-Statistics-Data-and-Systems/Statistics-Trends-and-Reports/MedicareMedicaidStatSupp/2013.html.

Note: Enrollment as of July 1, 2012. Totals may not add due to rounding. Data are the most recent comprehensive CMS information available.

Eligibility for Low-Income Assistance

Beneficiaries with limited incomes and resources may qualify for assistance with their Part D premiums, cost-sharing, and other out-of-pocket expenses. For 2013, an estimated 11.3 million Medicare beneficiaries received low-income subsidies (UIS). See **Table 2** below.

Table 2. Medicare Part D Low-Income Subsidy Enrollment Figures in Millions

	Medicaid, full dual eligible	Other, with full subsidy	Other, with Partial Subsidy	Total
2006	5.7	2.3	0.2	8.3
2007	5.9	3.0	0.3	9.2
2008	6.3	3.2	0.3	9.7
2009	6.4	3.3	0.3	10.0
2010	6.6	3.5	0.3	10.4
2011	6.6	3.7	0.3	10.6
2012	6.9	3.7	0.3	11.0
2013	7.1	4.0	0.3	11.5

Source: Medicare Trustees, *2014 Annual Report*, Table IV.B7.
Notes: Figures are for Calendar Years. Totals may not add due to rounding.

Full-Subsidy-Eligible Individuals

Certain groups of Medicare beneficiaries automatically qualify (and are *deemed eligible*) for the full low-income subsidy. So-called dual eligibles who qualify for Medicaid based on income and assets are automatically deemed eligible for Medicare prescription drug low-income subsidies. Additionally, those who receive premium and/or cost-sharing assistance from Medicaid through the Medicare Savings Program (MSP),[7] plus those eligible for Supplemental Security Income (SSI) cash assistance,[8] are automatically deemed eligible for low-income subsidies. This group includes all eligible persons who (1) have incomes below 135% of the federal poverty level, or $15,754.50 for an individual and $21,235.50 for a couple in 2014;[9] and (2) have resources below $8,660 for an individual and $13,750 for a couple in 2014.[10] The limits are increased annually by the percentage increase in the Consumer Price Index. (See **Table 3**.)

CMS deems individuals automatically eligible for LIS effective as of the first day of the month that they attain qualifying status (e.g., become eligible for Medicaid or SSI). The end date is, at a minimum, through the end of the calendar year within which the individual becomes eligible. Beneficiaries who are deemed LIS-eligible for any month during the period of July through December of one year are deemed eligible through the end of the following calendar year. CMS changes an individual's deemed status in mid-year only when such a change qualifies the beneficiary for a reduced co-payment obligation.

Eligibility for the LIS is not always continuous from year to year. For example, LIS beneficiaries who lose eligibility for Medicaid or SSI during the year are not automatically qualified to receive the LIS the next year. Each September, CMS notifies such individuals that their LIS-deemed status will end on December 31 of that year. Such individuals may reapply for the LIS, as they may qualify for the LIS through the application process. (See "LIS Enrollment.")

Table 3. Overview of How Medicare Beneficiaries Qualify for LIS

Eligibility	People with Medicare and Medicaid benefits	Basis	Eligibility Based On	Changes During the Year
Full-Subsidy Eligible	□ Full Medicaid benefits □ Partial Dual	Automatically qualify	State Files	□ Qualify for a fullcalendar year
	SSI benefits		SSA	□ Generally only favorable changes will occur within a year.
Other-Subsidy Eligible	Limited Income and Resources	Must apply	SSA (almost all) or states	□ Some events can impact status during a year. □ Subsidies can increase, decrease or terminate during a year.

Source: CRS table based on Social Security Administration (SSA) and CMS data.

At the end of each plan year, CMS reassigns LIS beneficiaries who are enrolled in Part D plans if their plan is terminated or raises its monthly premium to a level above the LIS benchmark premium for the plan region. The ACA altered the method for determining which Part D plans are eligible to enroll low-income beneficiaries so that more plans can qualify and, thus, reduce the number of low-income beneficiaries who are reassigned from year to year.[11] According to CMS, 516,405 LIS beneficiaries enrolled in PDP and MA plans were reassigned for 2014.[12]

Other-Subsidy-Eligible Individuals

Other individuals with limited incomes and resources who do not automatically qualify may apply for the low-income subsidy and have their eligibility determined by either the Social Security Administration (SSA) or their state Medicaid agency. This group includes all other persons who (1) are enrolled in a PDP plan or MA-PD plan; (2) have incomes below 150% of poverty, $17,505 for an individual and $23,595 for a couple in 2014; and (3) have assets below $13,440 for an individual and $26,860 for a couple in 2014[13] (increased in future years by the percentage increase in the CPI).

An individual who applies, and is deemed eligible for the LIS, is allowed to begin receiving benefits on the first day of the month in which the application was submitted. In most cases, this means that LIS status is applied retroactively. For example, if an LIS beneficiary was enrolled in a Part D plan prior to a determination of LIS eligibility, the Part D sponsor must ensure that the beneficiary is reimbursed for any premiums or cost-sharing that should have been covered by the subsidy. If a person wasn't already eligible for Medicare, the LIS subsidy takes effect on the first day of the month when his or her Medicare eligibility begins.[14]

Initial LIS eligibility determinations are for no longer than 12 months. If the SSA or a state Medicaid agency later decides that an individual is no longer eligible for the LIS, that same entity also decides when the LIS benefits end. The end date is always the last day of a calendar month, though it may occur in any month of the year.

Changes in LIS Status

LIS determinations are also reviewed in the case of certain developments that could affect the amount of the subsidy. Throughout each plan year, CMS uses state Medicare Modernization Act (MMA) and SSA files to initiate the eligibility process for new recipients, and look for any changes in eligibility status for current, low-income beneficiaries.[15]

The ACA created new rules for LIS redeterminations subsequent to the death of a spouse. Beginning in 2011, the surviving spouse of an LIS-eligible couple receives a grace period for a determination or redetermination of benefits.[16] For example, after the death of her husband, a widow would fill out and send a Part D redetermination form to CMS. After CMS reviews the document, if the information:

- indicates that the widow qualifies for a more generous subsidy or provides a higher resources limit, the change will take effect in the month following the month when the redetermination report was received;
- indicates no change in status, the widow will not be sent a redetermination form the following year (with some exceptions);
- indicates a need to reduce the LIS, or provide a less favorable resource limit, the redetermination would be postponed.

ENROLLMENT IN PART D

Enrollment Periods

A Medicare beneficiary who is signing up for Part D for the first time[17] may do so in one of three different enrollment periods, depending on the individual's circumstances:

- Initial Enrollment Period for Part D;
- Annual Open Enrollment Period (or Annual Coordinated Election Period, AEP); or
- Special Enrollment Period (SEP).

Individuals who qualify for LIS may enroll at any time.

Initial Enrollment Period

The initial enrollment period is the time during which an individual is first eligible to enroll in a Part D plan.[18] Beneficiaries not yet enrolled in Medicare may join a drug plan at any time during their seven-month initial Medicare enrollment period. The Part D initial enrollment period is the same as the enrollment period for Medicare Part B.[19] Coverage for new enrollees begins on the first day of the month following the month of enrollment, but no earlier than the first month they are entitled to Medicare.

Individuals who become eligible for Medicare but have "creditable" coverage," which is prescription drug coverage that CMS estimates will provide at least the same level of benefits as Medicare's standard prescription drug package, may choose not to sign up for Part D during the initial enrollment period. Sources of possible creditable coverage include some employer-based prescription drug coverage, including the Federal Employees

Health Benefits Program; qualified State Pharmaceutical Assistance programs (SPAPs); and military-related coverage (e.g., VA, TRICARE). However, these individuals could face a penalty if they let their creditable coverage lapse before enrolling in Part D. (See "Late Enrollment Penalty.")

Annual Open Enrollment Period

In general, an individual who does not sign up for Part D during his or her initial enrollment period may enroll only during the annual open enrollment period, held from October 15 to December 7 each year. Coverage then begins the following January 1. Beneficiaries already enrolled in a Part D plan may change their plans during the annual open enrollment period.

Beneficiaries may wish to change plans for a variety of reasons, including changes in their health status and prescription drug needs or in response to modifications by their plans. Generally, sponsors make changes to plan benefits effective at the beginning of each year. After the open enrollment period closes, most beneficiaries are locked into their Part D plans for the upcoming benefit year. Overall, about 13% of non-LIS Part D enrollees voluntarily changed plans in 2011.[20]

Special Enrollment Periods

There are a few, limited occasions when an individual may enroll in, or dis-enroll from, a Part D plan or switch from one Part D plan to another. These special enrollment periods (SEPs) are open to individuals who (1) move to a new geographic area,[21] (2) involuntarily lose creditable coverage, (3) receive inadequate information about their creditable coverage status, (4) are subject to a federal error, or (5) are enrolled in a PDP that has failed or has been terminated.[22]

Late Enrollment Penalty

A late enrollment penalty is assessed on persons who go without creditable drug coverage for 63 continuous days or more after the close of their initial enrollment period, and then sign up for Part D. The penalty is intended to encourage wider enrollment and prevent adverse selection, which can occur when healthy people put off buying insurance while those with a real or perceived need immediately enroll. If Part D enrollees are mainly sicker or have higher prescription drug costs, per-capita program costs can rise. Higher prices, in turn, may cause other enrollees (presumably healthier, less costly ones) to end coverage. Over time, if more persons drop out, program costs could become prohibitive.

The Part D late penalty is based on the number of months an individual does not have creditable coverage.[23] The penalty is calculated by multiplying 1% of the national base premium ($32.42 in 2014) by the number of full months an individual has been eligible but has been without coverage. The final amount is rounded to the nearest $0.10. For example, if a beneficiary was eligible for Part D in June 2011, but didn't sign up until the 2013 open enrollment period with coverage effective January 2014, and didn't have creditable coverage during the 30-month interim period, the individual would pay $9.70 more per month.[24]

The late penalty is applied permanently to Part D premiums. Because the national base premium is recalculated annually, and the penalty is based on the base premium, the penalty amount will increase in subsequent years if the base premium rises. Dual-eligible and other LIS beneficiaries are not subject to the late enrollment penalty.

Plan Selection

Sponsors can alter a plan benefit package at the beginning of a new program year, including changing the mix of drugs in a formulary and/or modifying required cost-sharing for certain drugs. Sponsors must mail an Annual Notice of Change (ANOC) to enrollees each year, to be delivered by September 30. The document describes any modifications to a plan's premiums, drug coverage, cost sharing, and other features for the coming benefit year. The delivery deadline is designed to ensure that beneficiaries have at least two weeks to review the information prior to October 15, the first day of the annual enrollment period.

Sponsors are required to send beneficiaries other enrollment-related materials and information such as the Summary of Benefits and Evidence of Coverage documents. These documents offer information about a plan's formulary, general utilization management and pricing policies, information on beneficiary rights, and other information.

Each year, Medicare beneficiaries should review the cost of their current drug and health plans, (if in MA) including premiums, co-pays, and deductibles, and compare the cost and coverage to other plans in their area. Additionally, beneficiaries should examine whether plans have price tiers that increase or decrease the price of the drugs they use, whether the plans offer preferred pharmacy options, and what, if any, utilization management requirements the plans impose for drugs. (See "Drug Utilization Management Programs.")

CMS posts information on its open enrollment web page to help beneficiaries compare Part D plan prices.[25] Beneficiaries, and persons assisting them, can also use the Medicare drug plan finder.[26] After a beneficiary enters information into the plan finder regarding medications being used, the dosages, and the pharmacy he or she plans to use, the plan finder displays Part D plans in the area that cover those particular drugs.[27] The plan finder also provides information on quality ratings to make it easier to compare plans based on cost, quality, and performance ratings.[28] CMS will send notices to beneficiaries in low-quality plans encouraging them to look at other, higher rated plans. (See "Low-Quality Plans.")

Information on plan availability and characteristics can be obtained from a number of additional sources, including the Medicare toll-free information number (1-800-MEDICARE), State Health Insurance Assistance Programs (SHIPs),[29] and other local organizations.

Low-Quality Plans

CMS uses a star-rating system to assess the quality of Part D plans.[30] MA-PD sponsors are rated on up to 48 quality and performance measures, while PDP sponsors are assessed on up to 15 measures. Plans are ranked on a scale of one to five stars, with five stars considered excellent. Part D Sponsors must provide star rating information to beneficiaries through a standard document that must be distributed with enrollment information and prominently posted on plan websites.[31]

CMS has determined that three stars is the lowest acceptable quality rating for a plan. CMS had announced that any Part D plan that failed to achieve at least an overall three-star rating for three consecutive years would be terminated from Part D, beginning in 2015.[32] In a September 8, 2014, memo to select Part D and MA plan sponsors, CMS said it would not exercise its authority to terminate contracts for 2015, but did intend to terminate contracts at the end of 2015 if plans did not achieve at least a three-star rating for 2016.[33] Part D enrollees are also provided with a special enrollment period in which they can switch to a five-star plan, provided they meet the plan's enrollment requirements.[34]

Non-renewal

About 3% of MA-PD enrollees and 0.1% of PDP enrollees were in Part D plans in 2012 that did not renew their contracts with CMS for the 2013 plan year. The share of such non-renewing plans has declined during the past several years. (See **Table 4**.)

Table 4. Non-renewing MA-PD and PDP Plans Share of Part D Beneficiaries Affected by Non-Renewing Plans

Year	Percent of MA Enrollees Affected*	Percent of PDP Enrollees Affected**	Percent of Total Enrollees Affected***
2011	9.9%	2.0%	4.8%
2012	2.5%	0.1%	1.1%
2013	3.0%	0.1%	1.3%

Source: Centers for Medicare & Medicaid Services, "2013 Medicare Part D Landscape."

Note: Note: * MA non-Renewing Enrollment/ MA Enrollment. ** PDP non-Renewing Enrollment / PDP Enrollment, ***Total non-Renewing Enrollment / Total Enrollment.

Plan Marketing

Plan sponsors are required to provide timely and accurate information in their marketing materials and are required to submit all annual enrollment marketing materials to CMS for review prior to mailing to enrollees.[35]

In general, Medicare marketing rules are designed to ensure that beneficiaries have complete and accurate information when making decisions about drug plans. For example, a plan that has received a four-star rating for one of the services it provides, but a three-star quality rating overall, cannot create promotional material stating that the plan is a four-star plan. Plans must use a standardized name and materials across their service region and must receive prior agreement from plan enrollees to provide information in a format other than a mailing. Plans are not allowed to market via unsolicited contacts, such as door-to-door sales. There are also limits on marketing and sales events, including presenting marketing materials to CMS for prior review. All plan sponsors must have interpreters in their call centers to translate for people who are not proficient in English.

Plans are required to provide certain documents upon request or enrollment, such as a summary of benefits, the plan formulary, and a directory of contracting pharmacies. Plan sponsors may offer nominal gifts (worth $15 or less) to potential enrollees, though they may not take the form of cash or rebates.[36]

Enrollment Process

Beneficiaries can join a Part D plan in a variety of ways[37] including (1) filling out a paper application; (2) visiting a plan's website and enrolling online; (3) using the Medicare online enrollment center at www.medicare.gov;[38] (4) calling the company offering the drug plan; or (5) calling 1-800-MEDICARE. In general, a PDP sponsor cannot deny a valid enrollment request from any Part D-eligible individual residing in its service area.

An individual (or his/her legal representative) must complete an enrollment request, and include all the information required to process the enrollment. Upon receiving an enrollment request, a PDP sponsor must provide, within 10 calendar days, (1) a notice of acknowledgement of receipt of the beneficiary's application, (2) a request for more information in cases of incomplete applications, or (3) a notice that the application has been denied, along with an explanation of the reasons why.

Prior to the effective date of enrollment, a plan sponsor must provide necessary information about being a member of the PDP, including the PDP rules and the member's rights and responsibilities. In addition, the PDP sponsor must provide the following: a copy of the completed enrollment form, if needed; a notice acknowledging receipt of the enrollment request providing the expected effective date of enrollment; and proof of health insurance coverage so that a beneficiary may begin using the plan services as of the effective date. For all enrollment requests, the PDP sponsor must submit the information necessary for CMS to add the beneficiary to its records as an enrollee of the PDP sponsor within seven calendar days of receipt of the compete enrollment request.

UIS Enrollment

Special enrollment rules apply to low-income individuals. Generally, there is a two-step process for low-income persons to gain Part D coverage.[39] First, a determination must be made that they qualify for the assistance; second, they must enroll, or be enrolled, in a specific Part D plan. Most LIS beneficiaries are permitted to switch plans throughout the year, unlike other Part D enrollees who generally may switch plans only during the annual enrollment period at the end of the year.

Auto-Enrollment

Full-benefit, dual-eligible individuals who have not elected a Part D plan automatically are enrolled into one by CMS.[40] CMS first uses data provided by state Medicaid agencies to identify full-benefit, dual-eligible individuals. CMS then identifies plan sponsors that offer at least one Part D plan in the region offering basic prescription drug coverage with a premium at or below the low-income premium subsidy amount. If more than one sponsor in a region meets the criteria, CMS auto-enrolls beneficiaries on a random basis among available PDP sponsors. CMS next identifies individual plans offered by the sponsor that include basic drug coverage with premiums at or below the low-income premium subsidy amount. The beneficiary is then randomly assigned among the sponsor's plans meeting the criteria.

If an individual is not eligible to enroll in a PDP because he or she is enrolled in a Medicare Advantage plan (other than a MA private-fee-for-service plan (MA-PFFS) that does not offer Part D, or a medical savings account (MSA) plan), CMS will direct the MA organizations to facilitate the enrollment of these individuals into an MA-PD plan offered by the same MA organization.

Some dual-eligible beneficiaries may find that they have been auto-enrolled in a plan that may not best meet their needs. For this reason, they are allowed to change enrollment at any time, with the new coverage effective the following month. If an enrollee selects a plan with a premium above the low-income benchmark, however, he or she is required to pay the difference.

Facilitated Enrollment

CMS established a process labeled "facilitated enrollment" for enrollees in Medicare Savings programs (MSPs), SSI enrollees, and persons who applied for and were approved for low-income subsidy assistance. The basic features applicable to auto-enrollment for dual eligibles (i.e., identification of eligibility through SSA and/or Medicaid data, random assignment to plans with premiums below the low-income benchmark, and assignment of MA enrollees to the lowest-cost MA-PD plan offered by the MA organization) are the same for facilitated enrollment.

Reassignment of Certain UIS Beneficiaries

Drug plans may increase premiums at the beginning of a plan year, in some cases raising them above the benchmark for LIS beneficiaries. When that is the case, CMS will reassign certain LIS recipients to different plans so they can continue to receive benefits without paying Part D premiums (or continue paying only a minimal amount). CMS may also automatically reassign LIS recipients if their current plan terminates operations. LIS beneficiaries who have voluntarily changed plans in previous years are not automatically reassigned by CMS, even if their plans charge premiums above the benchmark. LIS beneficiaries in MA-PD plans are automatically reassigned to PDP plans if their current plan ceases operations or they are affected by a reduction in the plan's service area.

About 1.8 million LIS beneficiaries were enrolled in benchmark PDPs in 2012 that had terminated or did not qualify as benchmark plans in 2013. CMS reassigned 516,405 beneficiaries to different PDPs for the 2014 benefit year. Another 1.2 million LIS beneficiaries were not reassigned because they had previously switched plans voluntarily.[41]

The 2010 ACA made changes to Part D in an effort to reduce the need for automatic reassignment of LIS beneficiaries. For instance, the law changed the methodology for calculating the benchmark premium for some plans. In addition, PDPs with premiums above LIS-eligible levels will not have their LIS beneficiaries reassigned if they voluntarily agree to waive a de minimis portion of the premium above the benchmark. However, such plans will not qualify to receive other LIS beneficiaries who are automatically reassigned from their current plans.[42]

PART D BENEFIT STRUCTURE

The MMA set out a standard prescription drug benefit structure. Plan sponsors may, and often do, offer different benefit designs and cost-sharing requirements, so long as they meet certain specifications. Under the standard benefit structure, with some exceptions, over the course of a year a beneficiary is responsible for paying (1) a monthly premium, (2) an annual deductible, and (3) co-payments or co-insurance for drug purchases. Additionally, for a certain period called the "coverage gap" (also known as the doughnut hole), beneficiaries face increased out-of-pocket costs. The ACA included provisions to gradually eliminate the coverage gap. (See "The Coverage Gap")

Actual costs to Part D beneficiaries vary from plan to plan, depending on the benefit structure and coverage offered; the costs and amount of drugs they use; and the level of any additional assistance, such as through a low-income subsidy.

Premiums

The majority of beneficiaries enrolled in Part D pay monthly premiums for Part D coverage. On average, beneficiary premiums represent roughly 25.5% of the cost of a standard Part D plan, as determined through annual bids submitted by insurers. (See "Standard Prescription Drug Coverage.") The beneficiary premium does not cover costs for federal reinsurance or subsidies to low-income beneficiaries. The dollar amount of Part D premiums will vary by plan.

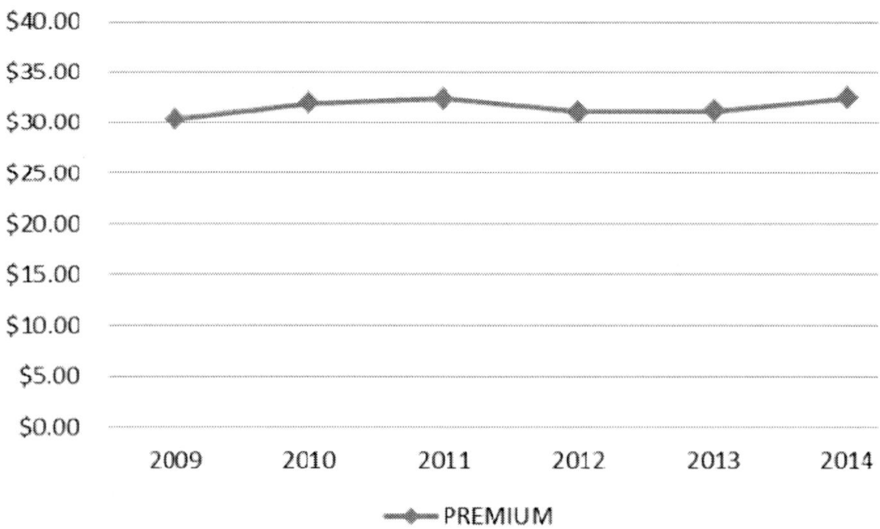

Source: Medicare Payment Advisory Commission, *March 2014 Report to Congress*, Table 14-15 and CMS "2014 Medicare Costs at a Glance."

Notes: Amounts reflect averages based on bids to provide basic Part D benefits.

Figure 1. Average Annual Part D Basic Monthly Premium.

Beneficiary premiums are based on average bids submitted by participating drug plans for basic benefits (the base beneficiary premium) each year and are adjusted to reflect the difference between a plan's standardized bid amount and the nationwide average bid. In 2014, the base beneficiary monthly premium is $32.42.[43] (See **Figure 1**.) Beneficiaries in plans with higher costs for standard coverage face higher-than-average premiums, while enrollees in lower-cost plans pay lower-than-average premiums for such coverage. Additionally, enrollees in MA-PD plans may have lower premiums if their plans choose to buy down, or reduce, the Part D premium.[44] The monthly premium is applied to all persons enrolled in a specific plan, except those who are receiving low-income subsidies or are subject to a late enrollment penalty. Beneficiaries may pay plans directly or have premiums deducted from their Social Security benefits.[45] Higher-income beneficiaries pay a monthly premium surcharge.

Premium Surcharge for Higher-Income Enrollees

When Part D began in 2006, all beneficiaries enrolled in the same plan (except those receiving the low-income subsidy) paid the same premium. Beginning in 2011, the ACA required Part D enrollees with higher earnings to pay higher premiums. The Part D requirements are similar to the income-based premium structure that was already in place for Medicare Part B.[46] Part D beneficiaries who have modified adjusted gross income (MAGI)[47] above set thresholds[48] are now assessed a special surcharge, referred to as an income-related monthly adjustment amount (IRMMA), in addition to their regular PDP or MA-PD plan premiums. According to the SSA, about 5% of Medicare enrollees are subject to the IRMMA.[49]

The higher-income surcharge is calculated as the difference between the Medicare Part D 25.5% base beneficiary premium and 35%, 50%, 65%, or 80% of the national average cost for providing Part D benefits, [50] excluding federal reinsurance or subsidies. The surcharge is based on beneficiary income, with higher-income beneficiaries facing a larger surcharge. Because individual plan premiums vary, the law specifies that CMS calculate the Part D surcharge using the base premium, rather than each beneficiary's individual premium amount.[51] (See **Table 5**.)

Beneficiaries pay the surcharge directly to the federal government, rather than to Part D plans. When applicable, IRMMA will be withheld from an enrollee's monthly Social Security check, Railroad Retirement benefit, or federal pension payment, unless the benefit check is not sufficient for the purpose.[52] If a beneficiary is directly billed for IRMAA, he or she has the option of paying through an electronic funds transfer or by other means. While the actual amount of the surcharge is recalculated annually, the income thresholds are fixed through 2019.

Table 5. 2014 Monthly Medicare Part D Surcharge for higher-income beneficiaries

If Annual Income in 2012 Was		Surcharge Calculation	2014 Payment Is
File Individual Tax Return	File Joint Tax Return		
$85,000 or less	$170,000 or less	Plan Premium	Plan Premium
Above $85,000 to $107,000	Above $170,000 to $214,000	(35%-25%)/25%	$12.10 + Plan Premium
Above $107,000 to $160,000	Above $214,000 to $320,000	(50%-25%)/25%	$31.10 + Plan Premium
Above $160,000 to $214,000	Above $320,000 to $428,000	(65%-25%)/25%	$50.20 + Plan Premium
Above $214,000	Above $428,000	(80%-25%)/25%	$69.30 + Plan Premium

Source: Medicare.gov, "Medicare 2014 Costs at a Glance" and CMS, "Annual Release of Part D National Average Bid Amount and other C & D Bid Related Information."

Note: Income figures refer to modified adjusted gross income.

Qualified Drug Coverage

Part D plan designs may vary, but all PDPs and MA-PDs must offer at least a minimum package of benefits. This minimum set, referred to as "qualified prescription drug coverage," may include either a standard package of prescription drug coverage established by Medicare or an alternative package that is actuarially equivalent.[53] Plans may also offer "enhanced" coverage that exceeds the value of standard coverage. Premiums for these enhanced plans are generally higher than for standard plans. According to CMS, in 2013, 4.5% of PDP plans were standard benefit plans, while 46.7% were actuarially equivalent plans, and 48.8% were enhanced alternative plans.[54] MA organizations offering MA-coordinated care plans are required to offer at least one plan for the service area that includes drug coverage. The drug coverage can be either basic coverage or enhanced coverage, with no premium for the supplemental benefits.[55]

Standard Prescription Drug Coverage

Under the standard Part D benefit, a beneficiary first pays a *deductible* ($310 in 2014). After the deductible has been met, the beneficiary is responsible for 25% of the cost of prescription drugs (with the plan covering the remaining 75%) up to the *initial coverage limi*t ($2,850 in 2014).

To reach the initial coverage limit in a 2014 standard plan, a beneficiary would pay the $310 deductible plus $635 in prescription costs, for total out-of-pocket costs of $945. The plan would pay the remaining $1,905.

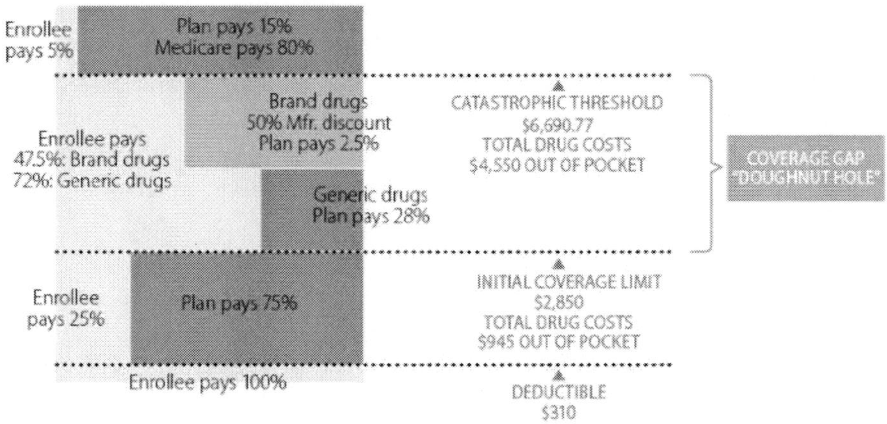

Source: Figure created by CRS based on data from CMS, Announcement of CY 2014 Medicare Advantage Capitation Rates and Medicare Advantage and Part D Payment Policies and Final Call Letter, Attachments IV and V.

Figure 2. 2014 Standard Medicare Prescription Drug Benefit.

After the initial coverage threshold has been reached, a beneficiary enters the *coverage gap* or "doughnut hole" and is responsible for a larger share of prescription drugs costs until he or she reaches the *catastrophic threshold*, which is about $6,690.77 in total drug costs in 2014.[56] Total spending in the coverage gap is about $3,840.77,[57] with a portion paid by the beneficiary, a portion covered by the plan, and a portion offset by manufacturer discounts for brand-name drugs. (See "The Coverage Gap.") Actual spending per beneficiary will vary depending on plan design (some enhanced plans provide additional subsidies in the coverage gap) and purchases of brand-name vs. generic drugs. However, when non-UIS beneficiaries reach total out of pocket spending of $4,550 in 2014, they have reached the catastrophic threshold. (See TrOOP.) Once the catastrophic threshold is met, plans may charge a beneficiary either a nominal, set co-payment for drugs or 5% coinsurance.[58] (See **Figure 2**.)

CMS uses a set formula to update annual Part D coverage parameters including the standard deductible, beneficiary total out-of-pocket amounts, and the initial coverage limit.[59] Annual percentage increases are based on average, per-capita spending for covered outpatient drugs for Medicare beneficiaries during the 12-month period ending in July of the previous year.

Actuarially Equivalent Plans

Plan sponsors have a number of options when designing pricing and benefits. Insurers may offer plans that provide the same level of coverage as the Part D standard plan, but may modify certain parameters and cost sharing such as the $310 deductible, while also imposing cost-sharing requirements that are higher than 25%. For example, nearly all plans use a tiered cost-sharing structure, where beneficiaries have a lower co-payment for generic drugs, and higher cost sharing for more expensive brand-name drugs. (See "Tiered Formularies.") As of February 2014, 43% of Part D enrollees in PDPs were in plans offering enhanced benefits, compared to 2% in standard plans and 55% in plans that were actuarially equivalent.[60]

Enhanced Plans

Insurers may also offer enhanced coverage that exceeds the value of defined standard coverage. Enhanced coverage includes basic coverage and supplemental benefits such as reductions in cost sharing and/or additional cost-sharing in the coverage gap. A PDP sponsor may not offer an enhanced plan unless it also offers a basic plan in the same region.

The structure of the Part D program, including the large number of plans available in each region, can make it complicated for beneficiaries to compare plans. The ACA required CMS to streamline the number of Part D plans in each region and simplify the enrollment process. Since the 2011 plan year, CMS has required Plan D sponsors that offer more than one plan per region to demonstrate that there are meaningful differences between their plans, in terms of premiums, cost-sharing, formulary design, or other benefits.[61] Plan sponsors may offer only one basic plan benefit design in a service area and no more than two enhanced plans in each service area. CMS determines whether there is a meaningful difference between plans, in part, by analyzing beneficiaries' potential out-of-pocket costs.

The Coverage Gap

One unique feature of the Medicare Part D drug benefit is the coverage gap—the period in which Part D enrollees are required to pay a larger share of total drug costs until they reach the catastrophic coverage level. Congress included the coverage gap in the benefit structure when it created the MMA in 2003 because the cost of continuous coverage would have exceeded goals for total spending.

As originally enacted, Part D provided a basic level of coverage for all beneficiaries, and extra protection for those with the highest drug costs (above the catastrophic limit). Part D enrollees who did *not* receive a low-income subsidy generally paid the full cost of drugs while in the coverage gap. The ACA includes provisions that will gradually phase out the coverage gap by 2020, at which point beneficiaries in standard plans will have a 25% cost-share from the time they meet a standard plan deductible until they reach the catastrophic limit, after which cost- sharing is reduced. (See "Phase Out of the Coverage Gap.")

Beneficiaries may have different levels of actual out-of-pocket spending in the coverage gap, depending on how their specific plans are structured and the percentage of brand-name and generic drugs that they use. Spending will also vary depending whether a beneficiary qualifies for the UIS based on his or her income and assets. For example, dual-eligible beneficiaries who are institutionalized have zero copays for drugs listed on a plan formulary, including during the time they are in the coverage gap. Other LIS beneficiaries have set-dollar co-pays while they are in the coverage gap.

According to CMS, about 28.2% of Part D enrollees reached their plans' initial coverage limit in 2010.[62] That figure includes 20.1% of non-LIS enrollees (18.4 million) and 41.3% of LIS enrollees (11.3 million). Part D plans are allowed to offer enhanced benefits in the coverage gap, though most do not. In 2013, about 21% of PDPs (244 plans) offered supplemental coverage in the coverage gap, and about 50% of MA-PD plans (809 plans) offered gap coverage.[63]

CMS offers enrollees suggestions for avoiding or delaying the coverage gap and for saving money while in the gap.[64] Strategies for minimizing out-of-pocket spending include switching to generic,[65] over-the-counter, mail-order, or other lower-cost drugs when possible; exploring national and community-based charitable programs or State Pharmacy Assistance Programs that might offer assistance;[66] and looking into Pharmaceutical Assistance Programs (also sometimes called Patient Assistance Programs) offered by pharmaceutical manufacturers.[67] Additionally, CMS suggests that beneficiaries continue using their Medicare drug plan cards even when in the coverage gap. Using the cards helps to ensure that beneficiaries are charged the drug plan's discounted, negotiated prices and that their out-of-pocket expenses count toward reaching the catastrophic coverage threshold.

Phaseout of the Coverage Gap

As required by the ACA, pharmaceutical manufacturers that want to participate in Medicare Part D must sign agreements to take part in the Medicare Coverage Gap Discount Program.[68] The program requires companies to provide a 50% discount on brand-name drugs for non-LIS Part D participants who are in the coverage gap. Drug makers began providing the brand-name discount in 2011.

Table 6. Closing the Doughnut Hole
Beneficiary Cost-Share Obligation While in the Coverage Gap

	Brand Name Drugs			**Generic Drugs**	
	Manufacturer Discount	Medicare Subsidy	Beneficiary Cost-Share	Medicare Subsidy	Beneficiary Cost-Share
2011	50%	0	50%	7%	93%
2012	50%	0	50%	14%	86%
2013	50%	2.5%	47.5%	21%	79%
2014	50%	2.5%	47.5%	28%	72%
2015	50%	5%	45%	35%	65%
2016	50%	5%	45%	42%	58%
2017	50%	10%	40%	49%	51%
2018	50%	15%	35%	56%	44%
2019	50%	20%	30%	63%	37%
2020	50%	25%	25%	75%	25%

Source: HHS Healthcare.gov, "Medicare Drug Discounts."

Notes: The manufacturer discount remains constant at 50% for brand-name drugs; the rest of the coverage comes in the form of escalating federal subsidies to Part D plans. The federal government provides the generic drug subsidy.

The federal government is providing additional subsidies for both brand-name and generic drugs purchased in the coverage gap. The federal government will eventually subsidize 25% of the cost of brand-name drugs and 75% of the cost of generic drugs purchased in the coverage gap. (Those enrollees who reached the coverage gap in 2010 received a $250 discount, in the form of a check.) (See **Table 6.**)

Participants in enhanced Part D plans that provide extra assistance in the coverage gap are to receive the ACA required discounts and government subsidies for any remaining amounts owed, in addition to their enhanced plan benefits.[69] For plan year 2014, non-UIS enrollees pay 47.5% of the cost of brand-name drugs, and 72% of the cost of generic drugs, while in the coverage gap. Manufacturers provide a 50% discount for brand-name products, while the federal government subsidizes 2.5% of the cost of brand-name drugs and 28% of the cost of generics.

In 2013, 4.6 million beneficiaries who were in the coverage gap received the 50% manufacturer discounts on brand-name drugs they purchased. The average discount per beneficiary was $930.50 with overall discounts totaling $4.2 billion.[70] The CBO has estimated that the net cost of closing the coverage gap will be $51 billion over 10 years (2013 to 2022).[71] (See **Figure 3**.)

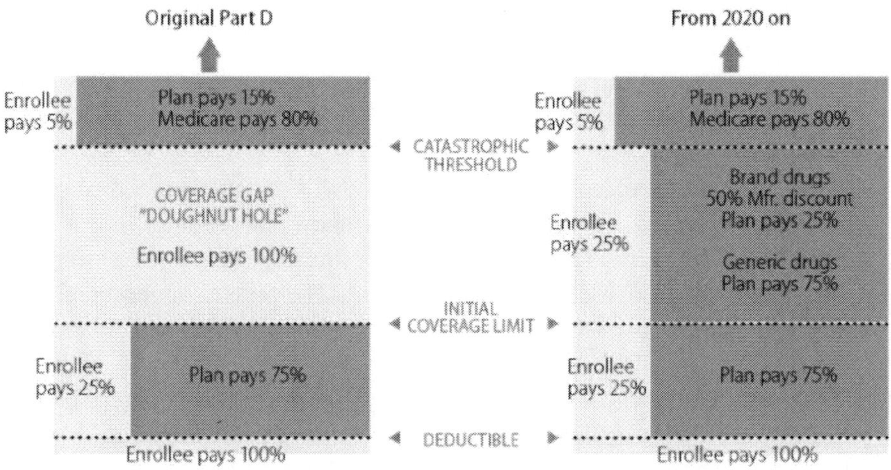

Source: Figure based on CRS analysis.

Figure 3. Closing the Doughnut Hole. The ACA includes provisions that will gradually close the doughnut hole by 2020.

True out-of-Pocket (TrOOP) Expenses

Beneficiaries must incur a certain level of out-of-pocket costs before catastrophic protection begins.[72] *Out-of-pocket costs are costs that are incurred by a beneficiary or are counted by CMS as incurred by a beneficiary*, including a plan deductible, cost-sharing up to the initial coverage limit, and the cost of certain drugs while in the doughnut hole, including the manufacturer subsidy.

Enrollee spending for Part D covered drugs is treated as a true-out-of-pocket (TrOOP) cost if it is:[73] paid by the enrollee (including a Medical Savings Account, Health Savings Account or Flexible Spending Account); paid by family members or friends; paid by a Qualified State Pharmacy

Assistance Program; covered by a low-income subsidy; paid by most charities; covered by a drug manufacturer discount under the Medicare coverage gap discount program; covered by the Indian Health Service;[74] or paid by an AIDs Drug Assistance Program.[75]

Examples of TrOOP Spending

Consider a non-LIS enrollee in a 2014 standard plan. In order to reach the initial coverage limit, the enrollee incurred TrOOP spending consisting of the $310 deductible and 25% coinsurance or copayments on total drug spending up to $2,850 ($635). The beneficiary now faces about $3,850.77 of spending in the doughnut hole before he or she reaches the catastrophic threshold.

While in the coverage gap, a beneficiary will pay 47.5% of the cost of brand-name drugs, including any pharmacy dispensing fees. The manufacturer will provide a 50% discount on the negotiated price of brand-name drugs, which will count toward TrOOP. The federal government will provide a subsidy of 2.5% of the cost of the drug, which will not count toward TrOOP.

A beneficiary who purchases generic drugs in the coverage gap will pay 72% of the cost of drugs, including pharmacy dispensing fees,[76] which will be counted toward TrOOP. The federal government will provide a 28% coverage subsidy that will not count toward TrOOP. In one example,[77] the beneficiary buys a brand-name drug that has a negotiated price of $60 and a $2 pharmacy dispensing fee. The total cost is $62. The beneficiary will pay 47.5% of the cost of the drug and dispensing fee ($62 x .475 = $29.45). The manufacturer will pay $30 (50% of the $60 negotiated price.) In this case, TrOOP will be $59.45 (The $29.45 beneficiary price, including a portion of the dispensing fee, plus the $30 manufacturer discount). The remaining $2.55, which is equal to 2.5% of the drug cost and 52.5% of the pharmacy dispensing fee, does not count toward TrOOP. In another example, the beneficiary buys a generic drug. The price for a generic drug is $20 and the dispensing fee is $2. The beneficiary will pay 72% of the cost of the generic drug plus the pharmacy fee ($22 x .72 = $15.84). The $15.84 will count as TrOOP. The government's 28% coverage portion will not count as TrOOP.

Incurred costs do not include Part D premiums; drugs that are not on a plan formulary; coverage by other insurance, including group health plans, workers' compensation, Part D plans' supplemental or enhanced benefits, or other third parties; or Patient Assistance Programs operating outside of Part D. Additionally, while the ACA manufacturer drug discounts count toward the TrOOP, federal subsidies for brand-name or generic drugs in the doughnut hole do not.

LOW-INCOME SUBSIDIES (LIS)

Medicare Part D provides subsidies to assist low-income beneficiaries with premiums and cost sharing. LIS cost sharing is linked to the standard prescription drug coverage and varies according to a beneficiary's assets and income and, also, whether a beneficiary is institutionalized, or is receiving community-based care. Full-subsidy eligibles[78] have no deductible, minimal cost sharing during the initial coverage period and coverage gap, and no cost-sharing above the catastrophic threshold. Additionally, full-benefit dual eligibles who are residents of medical institutions or nursing facilities have no cost-sharing. (See "Eligibility for Low-Income Assistance.")

Premium Assistance

Full-Subsidy-Eligible Individuals

Low-income beneficiaries who qualify for a full subsidy do not pay monthly plan premiums if they enroll in certain, lower-cost Part D plans. A PDP qualifies as a lower-cost or "benchmark" plan if it offers basic Part D coverage and charges premiums equal to, or below, a regional low- income premium subsidy amount calculated by CMS each year. (See "Availability of Low- Income Plans.") If a LIS beneficiary selects a plan with a premium that is higher than the regional benchmark, he or she must pay the extra cost.

Partial-Subsidy-Eligible Individuals

Subsidy-eligible individuals receive premium assistance based on an income sliding scale, as specified in **Table 7**.

Table 7. Sliding-Scale Premium for Subsidy-Eligible Individuals

Federal Poverty Level (FPL) and Asset Thresholds	Percentage of Premium Subsidy Amount
Income up to or at 135% FPL, with assets that do not exceed the calendar year resource	100%
limits for individuals or couples.	
Income above 135% FPL but at or below 140% FPL; assets that do not exceed the calendar	75%
year resource limits for individuals or couples.	
Income above 140% FPL but at or below 145% FPL; assets that do not exceed the calendar	50%
year resource limits for individuals or couples.	
Income above 145% FPL but below 150% FPL; assets that do not exceed the calendar year	25%
resource limits for individuals or couples.	

Source: SSA Program Operations Manual, Section HI 03030.025, "Resource Limits for Subsidy Eligibility," https://secure.ssa.gov/poms.nsf/lnx/0603030025.

Cost-Sharing Subsidies

Cost-sharing subsidies for LIS enrollees are linked to standard prescription drug coverage. Full- subsidy eligibles have no deductible, minimal cost sharing during the initial coverage period and coverage gap, and no cost sharing above the catastrophic threshold. Partial subsidy individuals have higher cost sharing. (See **Table 8**.) In addition:

- Full-benefit, dual eligibles who are residents of medical institutions or nursing facilities have no cost sharing, with some exceptions.[79] The ACA expanded the LIS subsidy so that beneficiaries receiving home and community-based services in lieu of institutional care also have no cost sharing.
- Other full-benefit, dual-eligible individuals with incomes up to or at 100% of poverty pay $1.20 for a generic drug prescription or preferred multiple-source drug prescription and $3.60 for any other drug prescription in 2014 up to the catastrophic threshold. They have no co-pays above the catastrophic limit.
- Full-subsidy-eligible individuals with incomes above 100% of poverty have cost-sharing for all drug costs, up to the catastrophic limit, of

$2.55 in 2014 for a generic drug or preferred multiple-source drug and $6.35 for any other drug (see **Table 10**).

- Partial-subsidy-eligible individuals have a $63 deductible in 2014, 15% coinsurance for all costs up to the catastrophic trigger, and cost-sharing above this level of $2.55 for a generic drug prescription or preferred multiple source drug prescription and $6.35 for any other drug prescription.

Each year, cost-sharing amounts for full-benefit dual eligibles below 100% of poverty are increased by the increase in the Consumer Price Index (CPI). The cost-sharing amounts for all other beneficiaries, and the deductible amount for other subsidy-eligible individuals, are increased by the annual percentage increase in per-capita beneficiary expenditures for Part D- covered drugs.

EMPLOYER SUBSIDIES

The MMA included provisions designed to encourage employers to continue to offer drug benefits to their Medicare-eligible retirees. Employers have a number of options for providing such coverage.

Retiree Drug Subsidy

Employers and union groups that provide prescription drug insurance to Medicare-eligible, retired workers may apply for federal retiree drug subsidies (RDS).[80] To qualify, an employer or union must offer drug benefits that are actuarially equivalent to, or more generous than, standard Part D prescription drug coverage. Sponsors must submit applications for CMS approval at least 90 days prior to the beginning of a plan year.

Table 8. Part D Standard Benefits, 2014
(by per capita drug spending category)

			Subsidy-Eligible Individuals			
	All Beneficiaries		Full-Subsidy Eligible		Other Subsidy Eligible	
Total drug spending (dollar ranges)	Paid by Part D	Paid by Enrollee	Paid by Part D	Paid by Enrollee	Paid by Part D	Paid by nrollee
$0 up to $310 Deductible	0%	$310	$310	0	$247	$63
Between Deductible and Initial Coverage Limit ($310.01-$2,850)	75%	25%	100% less enrollee cost- sharing	Institutionalized duals: $0 Duals up to or at 100% of poverty: $1.20/$3.60a Others: $2.55/$6.35b	85%	15%
Coverage Gap Between Initial Coverage Limit ($2,850) and Catastrophic Threshold (About $6,690.77)	52.5% for brand name drugs and 28% for generic drugs	47.5% for brand name drugs and 72% for generic drugs	100% less enrollee cost-sharing	Institutionalized duals: $0 Duals under 100% of poverty: $1.20/$3.60a Others: $2.55/$6.35b	85%	15%
Over Catastrophic Threshold	95%	5%c	100%	$0	100% less enrollee cost sharing	$2.55/$6.35b

Source: CMS, "Announcement of Calendar Year (CY) 2014 Medicare Advantage Capitation Rates and Medicare Advantage and Part D Payment Policies and Final Call Letter," http://www.cms.gov/Medicare/Health-Plans/MedicareAdvtgSpecRateStats/downloads/Announcement2014.pdf.

Notes:

[a] Maximum of $1.20 per prescription for generic or preferred drugs that are multiple source drugs; $3.60 per prescription for other drugs.

[b] Maximum of $2.55 per prescription for generic or preferred drugs that are multiple source drugs; $6.35 per prescription for other drugs.

[c] Minimum of $2.55 per prescription for generic or preferred drugs that are multiple source drugs; $6.35 per prescription for other drugs.

Medicare provides payments for eligible retirees, defined as individuals who are entitled to Medicare benefits under Part A and/or are enrolled in Part B, and who live in the service area of a Part D plan. An individual must be a retired participant in an employer- or union-qualified group health plan or the Medicare-enrolled spouse or dependent of a retired participant. A retiree health plan cannot receive a subsidy for a current worker or an individual who is enrolled in a Part D plan. (An employer or union does has the option of sponsoring its own Part D plan.)

For each retiree enrolled in a qualified plan in 2014, sponsors receive a federal subsidy equal to 28% of gross prescription drug costs between a threshold of $310 and a cost limit of $6,350.[81] The retiree subsidies are designed to encourage employers to maintain drug coverage, and have generally been less expensive for Medicare than enrolling these beneficiaries in a Part D drug plan. In 2013, the average annual RDS was about $569 per beneficiary.

Prior to enactment of the ACA, group health plans offering qualified drug coverage were eligible to receive the Medicare retiree health subsidy and, in addition, claim a federal tax deduction for the subsidy, along with the rest of the plan's spending on retiree health benefits. The ACA prohibits companies, beginning in 2013, from claiming a tax deduction for the Medicare drug subsidy.[82]

These changes, which will result in higher costs for retiree plans, are expected to prompt many employers to move away from the retiree drug subsidy program. The *2014 Medicare Trustees Report* predicts that the share of Medicare Part D beneficiaries covered by retiree drug subsidies will decline from 8%, of all Part D enrollees in 2013 to about 2%of Part D enrollees in 2023.[83]

Employer Group Waiver Plans

Though fewer employers are using the Part D retiree drug subsidy, a growing number of employers and unions are offering retirees (and their eligible spouses and dependents) Part D benefits through employer-group waiver plans (EGWPs). Under such arrangements a union or employer can:

- Elect to pay a portion of Part D premiums for eligible retirees.
- Elect to set up its own plan that supplements, or "wraps around" Part D coverage.[84]

- Contract with a PDP or MA-PD to offer standard Part D prescription drug benefits or enhanced benefits to Medicare-eligible retirees.
- Become a Part D plan sponsor.[85]

In general, federal subsidies to EGWPS mirror those for other Part D plans.[86] The Medicare trustees forecast that the number of individuals enrolled in EGWPs will rise from 15%, of Part D enrollees in 2013, to 19%, by 2023.[87]

DRUG COVERAGE

In order for a drug to be paid by Medicare's prescription drug benefit, it must be a drug that is covered under Part D and included in the formulary of an individual's Part D plan. (See "Formularies.") The MMA defines covered Part D drugs as (1) outpatient prescription drugs approved by the Food and Drug Administration (FDA), and used for a medically accepted indication; (2) biological products that may be dispensed only upon a prescription and that are licensed under the Public Health Service (PHS) Act and produced at a licensed establishment; (3) insulin (including medical supplies associated with the injection of insulin); and (4) vaccines licensed under the PHS Act. Drugs can also be treated as part of a plan's formulary as the result of a beneficiary coverage determination or appeal.

Certain drugs are excluded from Part D coverage by law, including drugs specifically excluded from coverage under Medicaid. The exclusion applies to (1) drugs used for anorexia, weight loss, or weight gain; (2) fertility drugs; (3) drugs used for cosmetic purposes or hair growth; (4) drugs for symptomatic relief for coughs and colds; (5) prescription vitamins and minerals; and (6) covered drugs when the manufacturer requires, as a condition of sale, that associated tests be purchased exclusively from the manufacturer. Drugs used for the treatment of sexual or erectile dysfunction are excluded from coverage unless they are used to treat another condition for which the drug has been approved by the FDA.

Some previously barred drugs are now covered. Since January 1, 2013, Part D plans have been required to include benzodiazepines in their formularies.[88] Barbiturates are also required to be included in plan formularies for an indication of epilepsy, cancer, or chronic mental health disorders. Effective in January 2014, the ACA removed smoking cessation agents, barbiturates and benzodiazepines from the list of drugs that may be excluded from Medicaid coverage. The ACA provisions mean that Part D restrictions on barbiturate coverage (i.e., limiting the drugs to treatment of epilepsy, cancer, or chronic mental health disorders) are ended. CMS does not, however, expect that many more drugs in this category will meet the "medically indicated" criteria allowing them to qualify for Part D coverage.[89]

If a state covers excludable drugs for Medicaid beneficiaries, it must also cover them for dual eligibles, in cases where the drugs are determined to be medically necessary. Dual eligibles may therefore receive coverage from Medicaid for some drugs that are excluded from Medicare.

Additionally, a Part D sponsor may elect to include one or more of these drugs in an enhanced Part D plan; however, no federal subsidy is available for the associated costs.

Drugs Covered by Other Parts of Medicare

Part D drug plans are prohibited from covering drugs covered by other parts of Medicare. This includes prescription medications provided during a stay in a hospital or skilled nursing facility that are paid for by the Part A program, and the limited circumstances when Part B covers prescription drugs. Part B-covered drugs include drugs that are not usually self-administered and are provided incident to a physician's professional services. These include such things as immunosuppressive drugs for persons who have had a Medicare-covered transplant; erythropoietin (an anti-anemia drug) for persons with end-stage renal disease; oral anti-cancer drugs; drugs requiring administration via a nebulizer or infusion pump in the home; and certain vaccines (influenza, pneumococcal, and hepatitis B for intermediate- or high-risk persons).

Formularies

Prescription drug plans operate formularies, which are lists of drugs that a plan chooses to cover and the terms under which they are covered. This means that plans can choose to cover some, but not all, FDA-approved prescription drugs.

A Part D sponsor's formulary must be developed and reviewed by a special CMS-approved Pharmacy and Therapeutics Committee.[90] A majority of the committee members must be practicing physicians or practicing pharmacists and the committees must each include one physician and one pharmacist who are experts in caring for elderly or disabled individuals. Committees are to base decisions on the strength of scientific evidence and standards of practice when developing and reviewing formularies. The committees should also take into account whether including a particular drug in a formulary (or in a particular tier of drugs) has therapeutic value in terms of safety and efficacy. The committees review prior authorization, step therapy, and other criteria limiting or managing access to drugs by Part D plan enrollees. (See "Drug Utilization.")

Formulary Categories and Classes

Formulary drugs are grouped into categories and classes of products that work in a similar way or are used to treat the same condition. The MMA required CMS to ask the United States Pharmacopeial Convention (USP) [91] to develop a list of categories and classes for plans and to periodically revise such classifications. A plan formulary must include at least two drugs in each category or class used to treat the same medical condition (unless only one drug is available in the category or class, or two drugs are available but one drug is clinically superior). The two-drug requirement must be met by providing two chemically distinct drugs. (Plans cannot meet the requirement by including two dosage forms or strengths of the same drug or a brand-name drug and its generic equivalent.)

Six Classes of Clinical Concern

In general, Part D drug plans are required to operate formularies that cover at least two drugs in each drug class. However, under CMS guidelines, Part D plans have been required to cover substantially all available drugs in the following six categories: immunosuppressant, antidepressant, antipsychotic, anticonvulsant, antiretroviral, and antineoplastic.[92] Plan sponsors have not been allowed to steer beneficiaries who are already using these drugs toward alternative therapies via policies such as requiring prior authorization or step-therapy mandates (see "Drug Utilization").[93] This policy was designed to mitigate the risk that drug therapy could be interrupted for vulnerable populations. Approximately 40% of Part D beneficiaries used a protected class drug in 2010, according to CMS.[94] Protected-class drugs made up 13% of all Part D prescription fills, and accounted for 18% of overall Part D drug costs in 2010.[95]

The Medicare Improvements for Patients and Providers Act of 2008 (MIPPA, P.L. 110-275) and the ACA both codified the general policy of creating protected classes, while directing the Secretary of HHS to spell out more specific criteria for identifying drug categories or classes of clinical concern.[96] As part of this process, the statutes allowed HHS to revamp the current protected classes and categories, including permitting Part D sponsors to exclude certain drugs from their formularies (or limit access to such drugs through utilization management or prior authorization restrictions).[97]

Vaccines

The Tax Relief and Health Care Act of 2006 (P.L. 109-432) required that Medicare drug plans, beginning in 2008, include all commercially available vaccines in their drug formularies, with the exception of vaccines covered under Medicare Part B. Medicare Part B generally covers vaccinations for influenza, pneumonia, and the Hepatitis B vaccine for intermediate to high-risk cases. Part B will also cover immunizations for patients exposed to an injury or disease, such as tetanus shots.[98] The Tax Relief and Health Care Act of 2006 also modified the definition of a Part D drug to require plans to cover the costs for administering Part D-covered vaccines, as well as the vaccine itself. CMS considers the negotiated price for a Part D vaccine to include the vaccine ingredient cost, a dispensing fee (if applicable), sales tax (if applicable) and a vaccine administration fee.[99]

CMS policy is that Part D vaccines, including administration costs, are to be billed on one claim. The policy applies to providers both in- and out-of-network. Unlike Part B vaccines, which are billed directly to Medicare, Part D claims are paid by the insurance provider; therefore the Part D entity/individual administering the vaccine may not be able to directly bill the Part D sponsor for the vaccine and administration. In some instances, patients must pay a physician for a vaccination up front, and then submit the bill to their insurance plan. CMS has issued guidance to plans regarding alternative billing options, such as allowing in-network pharmacists to administer vaccinations and to directly bill Part D, or having physicians electronically submit claims to Part D plans.[100]

Plan-Year Formulary Changes

Part D plans may alter their formularies from year to year. Plans are also allowed, in limited circumstances, to make changes to their formularies within a plan year.[101] Plans may not change therapeutic categories and classes of drugs within a plan year, except to account for new therapeutic uses or to add newly approved Part D drugs. If Part D plans remove drugs from their formularies during a plan year (or change cost-sharing or access requirements), they must provide timely notice to CMS, affected enrollees, physicians, pharmacies, and pharmacists.

Formulary changes may be made in the following circumstances:

- Plans may immediately remove drugs from their formularies that are deemed unsafe by the FDA or are pulled from the market by their manufacturers. Plans do not have to provide prior notice of such actions, but must provide retrospective notice to CMS and other affected parties.
- Plans may make formulary maintenance changes after March 1, such as replacing a brand-name drug with a new generic drug or modifying formularies as a result of new information on safety or effectiveness. These changes require CMS approval and 60 days' notice to appropriate parties.
- CMS will generally give positive consideration to formulary maintenance changes such as expanding formularies by adding drugs, moving a drug to a lower tier (thereby reducing copayments or coinsurance), or eliminating utilization management requirements.
- Plans may only remove drugs from a formulary, move covered drugs to a less- preferred tier status, or add utilization management requirements in accordance with approved procedures and after 60 days' notice to appropriate parties.[102] *Plans may make such changes only if enrollees currently taking the affected drugs are exempt from the formulary change for the remainder of the plan year.*

Transition Policies

CMS established transition standards to ensure that enrollees who move to a new plan do not abruptly lose coverage for their drugs—for example, in a case where a new plan does not cover a drug a beneficiary has been using. In such cases, a beneficiary can request that his or her physician check to see if the prescription can be switched to a similar drug on the new plan's formulary. If the physician determines that a specific drug is medically necessary, the doctor may request that the new plan make an exception to its policy.

Plans are required to continue a beneficiary's previous prescription during the first 90 days a beneficiary is enrolled in a new plan. Any refill must be for at least 30 days (unless the prescription is written for less than 30 days) for any drug not on the new plan's formulary. The requirement also applies to drugs that are on a plan's formulary, but which require prior authorization or step therapy.

DRUG UTILIZATION MANAGEMENT PROGRAMS

CMS regulations require that each Part D plan have an appropriate drug utilization management program that (1) includes incentives to reduce costs when medically appropriate, and (2) maintains policies and systems to assist in preventing over-utilization and under-utilization of prescribed medications.[103] Since the Part D program began in 2006, the trend among plans has been to impose greater cost-sharing and utilization management. In addition, during the past several years, CMS has imposed more stringent requirements on plans in an effort to identify possible program fraud and abuse involving certain prescription drugs. (See **Figure 4**.)

Tiered Formularies

Plan D plan sponsors may assign formulary drugs to tiers that correspond to different levels of cost sharing. In general, this structured pricing encourages use of generic medications by placing these medicines on the plan tier with the lowest out-of-pocket costs, and discourages the use of more expensive drugs by putting them on tiers that require higher out-of-pocket spending. Plans have flexibility in structuring the tiers. Different plans may place the same drug on different tiers, and drugs in parallel tiers may not have the same cost-sharing requirements. To illustrate, a five- tiered formulary may be structured so that Tier 1 includes preferred generics, Tier 2 includes non-preferred generics, Tier 3 contains preferred brand-name drugs, Tier 4 includes higher-cost, non- preferred brand names, and Tier 5 (the "specialty tier") has very expensive or rare drugs.[104]

Part D plans are permitted to institute a specialty tier for expensive products (e.g., unique drugs and biologics). Beneficiaries cannot appeal cost-sharing amounts for drugs placed on a specialty tier. Plans typically charge a percentage of the cost of a drug on the specialty tier (coinsurance), rather than a flat copayment. To ensure that beneficiaries dependent on specialty drugs are not "unduly discouraged" from enrolling in tiered plans, CMS has instituted the following conditions: (1) a plan may have only one specialty tier; (2) a plan with a standard deductible may impose coinsurance of up to 25% for specialty drugs, while a plan with a reduced or zero deductible may impose coinsurance of up to 33%;[105] and (3) only drugs with negotiated prices exceeding a set threshold may be placed on a specialty tier ($600 for a month's supply for 2014).[106]

Some Part D plan sponsors charge co-insurance of more than 33% for drugs on a non-preferred brand name formulary tier, up to the initial coverage limit.[107] According to CMS, best practices for developing formularies dictate that drugs are placed in a non-preferred tier only when drugs that are therapeutically similar (i.e., drugs that provide similar treatment outcomes) are in more preferable positions on the formulary. [108] CMS reviews plan sponsors' drug tier placement to ensure their formulary does not substantially discourage enrollment of certain beneficiaries, such as those with potentially high drug costs. Some of the largest Part D plans charge 50% co- insurance for non-preferred brand name drugs.[109]

According to CMS, 93% of PDPs had a specialty tier in 2013, down just slightly from 96% in 2012.[110] In addition, Part D plans are increasingly setting five or more tiers. In 2013, 70% of MA- PDs and 69% of PDPs had five or more tiers, compared to 29% and 33% respectively in 2010. About 0.25% of all 2013 Part D claims were for specialty tier drugs, but they accounted for about 11% of program spending.[111]

Other Drug Utilization Controls

Other utilization restrictions include (1) prior authorization, in which a beneficiary, with assistance of a prescribing physician, must obtain a plan's approval before it will cover a particular drug; (2) step therapy, where a beneficiary must first try a generic or less expensive drug to see if it works as well as the one prescribed; and (3) quantity limits, where the supply of drugs is initially limited to reduce the likelihood of waste (e.g., if a drug was not effective for a beneficiary or had intolerable side effects). A beneficiary who wants his or her plan to waive a utilization control must provide a physician statement indicating that a prescribed drug and dosage is medically necessary and providing a rationale as to why restrictions are not appropriate.

Starting in 2014, PDPs must apply a daily cost-sharing rate to prescriptions for less than a 30-day supply of medication (with some exceptions).[112] The daily cost-sharing rate is defined as the monthly co-payment under the enrollee's Part D plan, divided by 30 or 31 and rounded to the nearest lower dollar amount. The daily cost-sharing requirement gives beneficiaries an incentive to ask physicians for shorter prescriptions when trying a medication for the first time because the Part D sponsor will charge the lower, pro-rated cost sharing when the prescription is dispensed.[113] Shorter prescriptions could reduce Part D beneficiary costs and drug waste in cases where a prescribed drug is found not to be effective.[114]

		2010*	2011*	2012**	2013**
Prior Authorization	Total	12.5%	13.6%	14.4%	15.4%
	Brand	20.9%	22.0%	23.2%	25.2%
	Generic	5.8%	7.2%	7.5%	8.5%
Step Therapy	Total	2.2%	2.0%	1.8%	1.5%
	Brand	4.6%	4.4%	3.8%	3.3%
	Generic	0.3%	0.2%	0.3%	0.2%
Quantity Limits	Total	16.8%	18.4%	19.5%	21.0%
	Brand	26.1%	28.0%	27.6%	29.6%
	Generic	9.6%	11.1%	13.2%	15.0%

Source: CMS, "2013 Prescription Drug Plans."

Notes: * Brand/Generics are defined by the plan formulary. **Brand/Generics are defined by FDA-based Applicable/Non-Applicable definitions.

Figure 4. Utilization Controls in Part D PDP Plans. Average Percentage of PDP-Covered Drugs with Utilization Management Tools.

Part D Overutilization Monitoring

Recent investigations of the Part D program, including a 2011 Government Accountability Office (GAO) study, found that some beneficiaries had obtained overlapping prescriptions from multiple physicians for frequently abused prescription drugs.[115] A separate CMS study of contract year 2011 data found that about 225,000 Part D beneficiaries, or 0.71% of all Part D beneficiaries, had exceeded recommended thresholds for opioid use for 90 or more consecutive days.[116] Of this group, nearly 64,000 filled opioid prescriptions written by at least four prescribers, and 8,460 had at least eight prescribers. The HHS Office of Inspector General (OIG) also found other cases of potential overprescribing and overuse of certain prescription drugs.[117]

To reduce the potential for inappropriate utilization of opioids and acetaminophen in the Part D program, CMS instructed[118] plan sponsors to make several improvements to their formulary management processes by January 1, 2013, including:

- Appropriate controls at the point of sale to limit access to medications containing opioids or acetaminophen, as well as quantity limits to guard against over- utilization of drugs.
- Improved review of filled prescriptions to identify at-risk beneficiaries.
- Case management with the beneficiaries' prescribers.
- Data-sharing between Part D sponsors when a beneficiary with a prescription drug claim that is under review moves from one Part D plan to another.

CMS also implemented a Medicare Part D Overutilization Monitoring System (OMS)[119] to more closely track whether sponsors had adequate systems to identify beneficiaries who may be over- utilizing prescribed drugs. CMS each quarter provides Part D sponsors with reports of beneficiaries identified as having potential overutilization issues. Plan sponsors must develop criteria to identify which beneficiaries should be subject to special case management, and must notify CMS of the status of each beneficiary's case.

In May 2014, CMS issued final rules designed to further combat overuse and abuse of Part D drugs.[120] The regulations require that, beginning in June 2015, physicians and other health care professionals must be enrolled in the Medicare program or have a valid record of opting out of Medicare in order to prescribe drugs under Medicare Part D. CMS may revoke Medicare enrollment for physicians or other professionals determined to have a prescribing pattern that is "abusive, represents a threat to the health and safety of Medicare beneficiaries, or otherwise fails to meet Medicare requirements." CMS also may revoke Medicare enrollment if a prescriber's Drug Enforcement Administration (DEA) Certificate of Registration is suspended or revoked, or if his or her ability to prescribe drugs is revoked by any state in which he or she practices.

Medication Therapy Management

Part D plans (with some exceptions) must include a Medication Therapy Management Program (MTM), which is a system of coordinated pharmacy care for patients with multiple medical conditions who may be seeing a series of practitioners. A MTM includes medication reviews, patient consultation and education and other services. Each plan's program must be reviewed and approved annually by CMS, and is one of several, required elements that is considered when CMS evaluates a sponsor's bid to participate in the Part D program for an upcoming contract year.

For plan year 2014, Part D sponsors must automatically enroll beneficiaries in a MTM program if they meet the following criteria: (1) they have multiple chronic diseases, with three being the maximum that can be required; (2) they are taking at least two to eight Part D drugs; and (3) they are likely to have annual covered drug costs that exceed $3,017.[121]

Part D sponsors also may target beneficiaries with any chronic diseases, or with specific chronic diseases. If plans target beneficiaries with specific diseases, they must include at least five of which CMS has defined as nine core chronic conditions:[122]

- Alzheimer's Disease;
- Chronic Heart Failure;
- Diabetes;
- Dyslipidemia;
- End-Stage Renal Disease (ESRD);
- Hypertension;
- Respiratory Disease (such as asthma or chronic lung disorders);
- Bone Disease-Arthritis;
- Mental Health (such as depression, schizophrenia, or bipolar disorder).

CMS guidelines state that, once enrolled, beneficiaries should remain in a MTM program for the course of a plan year, even if they no longer meet one or more of the eligibility criteria. The MTM program must include a comprehensive review of a beneficiary's medications, intervention with both beneficiaries and prescribers, and quarterly, targeted medication reviews.[123]

PART D PLANS: PAYMENT AND PARTICIPATION

Medicare Part D participants must obtain coverage through a private insurer, or other entity, that contracts with Medicare (a plan sponsor). As previously described, beneficiaries may select either a stand-alone prescription drug plan or a Medicare Advantage plan that includes prescription drug coverage along with other Medicare services.[124]

PDPs are required to be available, region-wide within each of the 34 designated PDP regions. MA-PDs are generally local, operating on a countywide basis; however, region-wide MA-PDs are available in many of the 26 MA regions in the United States. A PDP sponsor may offer a PDP in more than one region, including all PDP regions; however, the sponsor must submit separate coverage bids for each region it serves.[125] According to CMS, there were 22 national PDPs run by 11 parent organizations in 2013, compared to 24 national PDPs from 11 parent organizations in 2012.[126] Medicare payments to plans are determined through a competitive bidding process, and enrollee premiums are tied to plan bids. Plans bear some risk for their enrollees' drug spending.

Approval of PDP Plans

Each year, CMS issues a Call Letter to sponsors planning to offer PDP and/or MA plans in the following year. The 2014 Call Letter, issued on April 1, 2013, combined updated contracting guidance and payment information for both programs.[127]

Potential PDP and MA sponsors are required to submit bids by the first Monday in June of the year prior to the plan benefit year. The following information must be included as part of the bid: (1) coverage to be provided; (2) actuarial value of qualified prescription drug coverage in the region for a beneficiary with a national average risk profile; (3) information on the bid, including the basis for the actuarial value, the portion of the bid attributable to basic coverage and, if applicable, the portion attributable to enhanced coverage, and assumptions regarding the reinsurance subsidy; and (4) service area. The bid also includes costs (including administrative costs and return on investment/profit) for which the plan is responsible. The bid must exclude costs paid by enrollees, payments expected to be made by CMS for reinsurance, and any other costs for which the sponsor is not responsible. CMS reviews the information when negotiating with plan sponsors and deciding whether to approve their program bids.

CMS may approve a drug plan only if certain requirements are met. For example, CMS must determine that the plan and sponsor meet requirements relating to actuarial determinations and beneficiary protections. The plan cannot be designed in a way (including any formulary or tiered formulary structure) that would likely discourage enrollment by certain beneficiaries.

If their bids are approved, PDP sponsors enter into 12-month contracts with CMS. A contract may cover more than one Part D plan. Under the terms of a contract, the sponsor agrees to comply with Part D requirements and have satisfactory administrative and management arrangements.

Non-interference Provision

The MMA, which created the Part D program, contains a provision that states that the Secretary may not interfere in negotiations on drug prices nor set plan formularies. The actual wording of the so-called non-interference provision is that: "In order to promote competition under this part and in carrying out this part, the Secretary: (1) may not interfere with the negotiations between drug manufacturers and pharmacies and PDP sponsors; and (2) may not require a particular formulary or institute a price structure for the reimbursement of covered Part D drugs."[128]

Plan Availability

Part D sponsors offered 1,065 standalone PDP plans for 2013, an increase of two plans from 2012.[129] There were 2,350 MA-PD plans offered in 2013, an increase from 2,116 the previous year and from 1,657 in 2006.[130] (See **Figure 5.**)

Each PDP region, on average, had 15 enhanced standalone plans and 16 basic plans, compared to an average of 17 enhanced plans and 20 basic PDP plans per region in 2006 when the Part D program began operation. PDP enrollment has been concentrated among a relatively small number of sponsors. For example, in 2013 the nine largest nationwide PDPs accounted for nearly 60% of PDP enrollment. UnitedHealth Group's AARP Rx Preferred had 17% of PDP enrollment, followed by CVS SilverScript Basic with 12% and Humana/Walmart Preferred and Enhanced Rx Plans with 12%.[131]

Availability of Low-Income Plans

A Part D plan qualifies as a LIS benchmark plan if it offers basic Part D coverage and charges premiums that are equal to, or lower than, the average, regional low-income benchmark premium. Regional LIS benchmark premiums are recalculated annually, based on the weighted average of all premiums in each of the 34 PDP regions. The formula for determining the benchmark is based on premiums for basic prescription drug coverage, or the actuarial value of basic prescription drug coverage for plans that offer enhanced coverage. For MA-PD plans, the formula uses the portion of the premium attributable to basic prescription drug benefits.

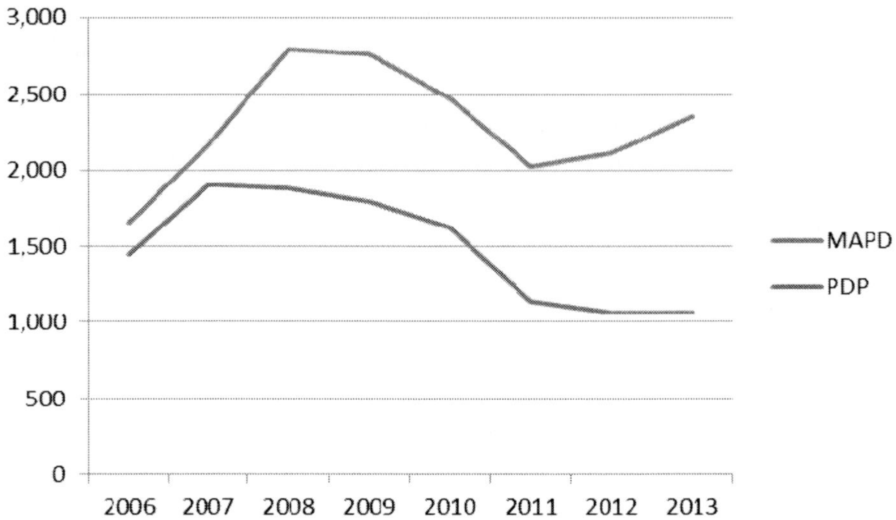

Source: CMS, "2013 Medicare Part D Landscape."

Notes: CMS in 2010 issued regulations requiring Part D sponsors to illustrate substantial differences between plans in order to offer multiple plans in a region. The regulations affected the number of plans offered.

Figure 5. Medicare Part D Plans, by Year. Number of PDP and MA-PD Plans Offered Annually.

Each PDP region had at least two LIS plans in 2013, with an average of 10 LIS plans in each region, according to CMS.[132] LIS beneficiaries enrolled in a plan that loses its benchmark status for a coming plan year are either automatically enrolled in a new plan by CMS or must select a new plan to avoid paying premiums and other cost-sharing requirements. (See "LIS Enrollment.")

Plan Payments

Medicare provides a subsidy for each non-LIS Medicare enrollee in a Part D plan that is equal to 74.5% of average, standard coverage. The average subsidy takes two forms: *direct subsidy payments* and *reinsurance payments*. Medicare also establishes *risk corridors* to limit a plan's overall losses or profits. In addition, Medicare pays most of the cost-sharing and premiums for LIS beneficiaries enrolled in PDP or MA-PD plans.

Direct Subsidies

Medicare makes monthly prospective payments (direct subsidies) to plans for each Part D enrollee. The payments are based on the nationwide average of plan bids for providing basic drug coverage,[133] weighted by the plans' share of total enrollment.[134] (The national average monthly bid is $75.88 for plan year 2014.)[135] The subsidy amount is risk-adjusted to account for the health status of the beneficiaries expected to enroll; plans with sicker enrollees receive a higher subsidy. The subsidy is further adjusted to cover expected, additional costs associated with LIS enrollees. Lastly, the payment is reduced by the base beneficiary premium for the plan. (See "Premiums.")

Reinsurance Subsidies

As previously noted, in a standard drug plan, the Part D sponsor pays nearly all drug costs above a catastrophic threshold, except for nominal beneficiary cost sharing. (See "Part D Benefit Structure.") Medicare subsidizes 80% of each plan's costs for this catastrophic coverage – the reinsurance subsidy. Payments are made on a monthly basis during the year, based on either estimated or incurred costs, with final reconciliation made after the close of the year.

Risk Corridor Payments

The MMA also established risk corridors for Part D plans. Under the risk corridors, Medicare limits plan sponsors' potential losses, or gains, by financing some higher-than-expected costs, or recouping excessive profits. Risk corridors are based on a plan's allowable costs (spending) relative to a percentage of its target amount (revenues), as defined below:

- Allowable costs are defined as costs (excluding administrative costs, but including costs directly related to drug dispensing) incurred by a plan sponsor or organization that are actually paid (net of discounts, chargebacks, and average percentage rebates) by the sponsor or organization. Plans may not include costs for benefits beyond the Part D basic benefit amount. The costs are reduced by the sum of reinsurance payments and low-income subsidy payments.[136]
- The target amount is defined as total payments to a plan (including amounts paid by both Medicare and enrollees) based on a plan's standardized bid[137] for offering the Part D drug benefit, as risk adjusted. The target amount does not include administrative expenses assumed in the plan's standardized bid.[138]

At the end of each year, the target amount is compared to the plan's actual, allowable costs.[139] If actual costs exceed the target, Medicare reimburses the plan for a portion of its losses. If costs are below the target, the sponsor may be required to refund money to CMS. As CMS has gained more experience with Part D, the risk corridors have widened, increasing the share of insurance risk borne by the plans. From 2008 to 2011, drug plans bore all gains and losses that fell within 5% of expected costs, compared with a smaller range of 2.5% of expected costs in 2006 and 2007. (See **Table 9**.)

Table 9. Plan Liability Under Risk Corridor Provisions

Risk Corridor	Plan Liability for Costs Above and Below Target
2006-2007	
Costs below 95% of target	80% refund
Costs between 95% and 97.5% of target	75% refund
Costs between 97.5% and 102.5% of target	Full risk
Costs between 102.5% and 105% of target	Risk for 25% of amount
Costs over 105% of target	Risk for 20% of amount
2008-2015	
Costs below 90% of target	80% refund
Costs between 90% and 95% of target	50% refund
Costs between 95% and 105% of target	Full risk
Costs between 105% and 110% of target	Risk for 50% of amount
Costs over 110% of target	Risk for 20% of amount

Since 2012, CMS has had the authority under the MMA to either leave the corridors unchanged or to widen them. CMS has moved to keep the corridors at 2011 levels through the 2015 program year.[140] CMS does not have the authority to narrow the risk corridors. (See **Table 10**.)

Table 10. Medicare Part D Risk Corridor Payment Increases and Decreases In Billions of Dollars

Year	Risk Sharing Payments
2007	-$0.7
2008	-$1.3
2009	-$0.1
2010	-$0.7
2011	-$1.0
2012	-$0.8
2013	-$1.1
2014	-$0.2a

Source: The 2014 Annual Report of the Boards of Trustees of the Federal Hospital Insurance and Federal Supplementary Medical Insurance Trust Funds, Table IV.B10, http://www.cms.gov/Research-Statistics-Data-and- Systems/Statistics-Trends-and-Reports/ReportsTrustFunds/downloads/tr2014.pdf.

Notes: Positive amounts represent payments from CMS to Part D insurers, while negative amounts represent net payments from the plans to CMS. The amounts may include the delayed settlement of risk sharing from prior years.

[a] 2014 is an estimate; other years are actual data.

Reconciliation

Following the close of a calendar year, CMS makes retroactive adjustments to the direct subsidy payments made to plans to reflect actual plan experience. The direct subsidy payments are adjusted based on updated data about actual beneficiary health status and enrollment. Additionally, prospective payments for reinsurance and low-income subsidy payments are compared to actual incurred costs, net of any direct or indirect remuneration (including discounts, chargebacks or rebates), and other related data, and appropriate adjustments are made to the plan payments. Finally, any necessary adjustments are made to reflect risk sharing under the risk corridor provisions.

In general, Part D plans have tended to overestimate their costs for operating Part D plans. For example, in 2013 Part D plans made about $1 billion in risk corridor payments to CMS.[141] CMS data on individual plans show considerable variation in terms of risk-sharing, with some plans making significant risk corridor payments to CMS, and others requiring payments from the government.[142]

PHARMACY ACCESS AND PAYMENT

Part D sponsors are required to establish a pharmacy network sufficient to ensure access to covered Part D drugs for all enrollees.[143] Sponsors must demonstrate that they provide (1) convenient access to retail pharmacies for all enrollees, (2) adequate access to home infusion pharmacies for all enrollees, (3) convenient access to long-term care (LTC) pharmacies for residents of LTC facilities, and (4) access to Indian Health Service, Tribes, or Urban Indian Programs pharmacies operating in the sponsor's service area.[144]

Any Willing Pharmacy

Part D sponsors are required to permit any pharmacy that is willing to accept the sponsor's standard contracting terms and conditions to participate in the plan's network, including mail- order pharmacies.[145] A sponsor's standard terms and conditions, particularly reimbursement terms, may vary to accommodate geographic areas or types of pharmacies, so long as all similarly situated pharmacies are offered the same standard terms and conditions. A Part D sponsor may not require a network pharmacy to accept insurance risk as a condition of participation in its pharmacy network.

Preferred Pharmacy

While any qualified pharmacy can participate in a plan network, Part D plans, with the exception of plans offering defined, standard coverage,[146] may contract with a smaller subset of pharmacies, or pharmacy chains, to serve as preferred pharmacies.[147] Preferred pharmacies generally are marketed as having lower beneficiary cost-sharing than other pharmacies in the plan network. Beneficiaries who sign up for a preferred pharmacy plan still have the option of going to any one of a number of network pharmacies in their plan region, but may face a higher cost-share to fill a prescription at a non-preferred pharmacy.

The creation of a preferred pharmacy network must not increase overall CMS payments to a Part D plan.[148] In addition, the cost differential between preferred and non-preferred pharmacies cannot be set at a level that discourages enrollees in certain locations, such as inner cities or rural areas, from enrolling in a Part D plan.

The number of Part D plans offering preferred pharmacy options has risen rapidly during the past several years. Half of PDP enrollees in 2013 were enrolled in plans that offered preferred networks, some including large pharmacy chains.[149] The growth of the preferred pharmacy networks has raised concerns among some smaller pharmacies, and has led to increased scrutiny from CMS. CMS in its final 2014 Call Letter[150] indicated that an initial review of its data found that aggregate unit drug costs may be higher in preferred networks in some plans, and reminded sponsors that marketing materials for such plans must be clear and accurate.[151]

Retail Pharmacy Access

To ensure that enrollees have convenient access to covered drugs, Part D networks must include a sufficient number of pharmacies that dispense drugs directly to patients (other than by mail order).

CMS defines convenient access as follows:

- In urban areas, at least 90% of Medicare beneficiaries in a Part D sponsor's service area, on average, live within two miles of a retail pharmacy participating in the sponsor's network.
- In suburban areas, at least 90% of Medicare beneficiaries in the sponsor's service area, on average, live within five miles of a retail pharmacy participating in the sponsor's network.
- In rural areas, at least 70% of Medicare beneficiaries in the sponsor's service area, on average, live within 15 miles of a retail pharmacy participating in the sponsor's network.[152]

Mail-Order Pharmacy Access

Part D plans have the option of including mail order pharmacies in their networks, though they cannot count such pharmacies in meeting retail pharmacy access requirements.[153] Plan sponsors may direct enrollees to buy certain formulary drugs (such as a particular tier of drugs or maintenance drugs) through a mail-order pharmacy. If a Part D plan instructs enrollees to use mail-order pharmacies for certain purposes (i.e., filling a 90-day prescription), it must make sure they have reasonable access to the same benefits at retail pharmacies. Enrollees may be charged more by Part D sponsors for filing certain prescriptions at a retail pharmacy, within certain limits set by CMS.[154]

Long-Term Care Pharmacy Access

Part D sponsors must offer LTC pharmacy access to beneficiaries in LTC facilities. In meeting this requirement, plan sponsors must offer standard long-term care (LTC) pharmacy network contracts to all LTC pharmacies operating in their service area that request such contracts. The pharmacies must be able to meet performance and service criteria specified by CMS, as well as any standard terms and conditions established by the Part D sponsor for its network LTC pharmacies. Part D sponsors may not rely on out-of-network pharmacies to meet the LTC convenient access standards.

Home Infusion Pharmacy Access

Part D covers certain home-infusion drugs, which are prescription drugs that are given intravenously in a home setting. Administration of the drugs may require tubing and catheters or special pumps. Part D plan sponsors must be able to deliver home-infusion drugs to plan enrollees within 24 hours after the enrollees are released from an acute care setting, unless the next dose of the medication is not due to be taken for more than 24 hours. (An acute care setting is a hospital, ambulatory care unit or similar facility where a patient receives treatment for a serious but brief illness). Part D plans are not expected to pay for supplies, equipment or professional services needed for home infusion therapy. They are expected to stock drugs in a form that can be easily used, to deliver products when needed, and to ensure that enrollees have the necessary supplies and professional assistance before dispensing home infusion drugs.

MedPAC, in a 2012 report requested by Congress, laid out two possible approaches for improving access to home infusion: (1) filling in gaps in current coverage (such as the need for greater access to supplies, nursing and equipment for patients), and (2) creating a demonstration project to evaluate a more integrated benefit combining pharmacy and medical coverage, for beneficiaries needing infused antibiotics.[155]

Out-of-Network Access

In general, a beneficiary must go to a pharmacy in his or her Part D network. However, in cases where enrollees cannot reasonably be expected to obtain covered drugs at a network pharmacy, and when such cases are not routine, a Part D plan must ensure that enrollees have adequate access to out-of-network pharmacies.[156] One example would be if a Part D enrollee were traveling in the United States, came down with an illness, and needed to have a prescription filled. Another possible scenario would be a federal disaster declaration in the case of major storm or other event, where a beneficiary was not able to use an in-network provider.

Part D plans must craft reasonable guidelines for out-of-network usage, and can set conditions such as requiring enrollees to order maintenance-type drugs from a mail-order pharmacy if they are going to be traveling for an extended period of time. In general, plans may not routinely allow more than a month's worth of medication to be dispensed at an out-of-network pharmacy. Enrollees will likely be required to pay more for a covered Part D drug purchased out of the plan network than one purchased at a network pharmacy.

Payments to Pharmacies

Plan sponsors negotiate with pharmacies to include a sufficient number and geographic distribution of pharmacies in their networks. A plan reimburses a pharmacy for the cost of a drug, plus a dispensing fee. Pharmacies set their own rates for dispensing drugs but may give a plan a discount from their usual rate.

The law requires Part D sponsors to make payment for "clean claims," within 14 calendar days of the date when an electronic claim is received, and within 30 calendar days of the date that non- electronically submitted claims are received.[157] A clean claim is a claim that does not require further development or investigation (for example, has all required documentation) or other special treatment that would prevent the claim from being paid in a timely manner. If payment is not issued, mailed, or otherwise transmitted within the applicable number of calendar days after a clean claim is received, the PDP sponsor or MA-PD plan will be required to pay interest to the pharmacy that submitted the claim.

COVERAGE DETERMINATIONS, APPEALS, AND GRIEVANCES

Part D enrollees have the right to appeal coverage determinations, file grievances against plan sponsors, and file complaints regarding quality of care.[158] PDPs and MA-PDs are required to provide enrollees with written information about their rights, and to institute both standard and expedited procedures for addressing coverage issues.[159]

An enrollee may appoint a representative to act on his or her behalf during the grievance and appeals process such as a friend, relative, attorney, physician, or an employee of a pharmacy or a charity. To appoint a representative, an enrollee must submit a written statement to the drug plan sponsor.[160] Alternatively, a surrogate or representative may be appointed by a court or authorized under a state or other applicable law to act on behalf of an enrollee. A prescribing physician or other prescriber may request a standard or expedited coverage determination, redetermination, or independent review entity (IRE) reconsideration on behalf of an enrollee without being named a representative.[161] (Physicians or prescribers do not have all the rights of a designated representative, however, unless they have gone through the formal appointment process.)

Coverage Determination

A coverage determination is any decision (whether an approval or denial) made by a plan sponsor with regard to covered benefits. Examples of coverage determinations include 1) a decision about whether to provide or pay for a Part D drug that an enrollee believes may be covered;[162] 2) a decision concerning a request about a specific drug payment tier;[163] 3) a decision concerning a request to cover a drug that is not included on a plan formulary;[164] 4) a decision regarding cost- sharing levels; or 5) a decision regarding whether an enrollee has satisfied a prior authorization or other utilization management requirement. An enrollee, an enrollee's appointed representative, or his or her physician may file a request for a coverage determination.[165]

An enrollee may also request an expedited decision regarding a drug that has not already been furnished. The plan must make a decision within 24 hours in cases where using the standard timeframe may seriously jeopardize the life or health of the enrollee or the enrollee's ability to regain maximum function. A Part D sponsor that approves a request for expedited determination must make its determination and notification, whether adverse or favorable, as expeditiously as the enrollee's health condition requires, but no later than within 24 hours.

If a Part D plan sponsor denies a request for an expedited determination it must:[166]

- Make the determination within the 72-hour timeframe established for a standard determination; and
- Give the enrollee and prescribing physician or other prescriber prompt oral notice of the denial.

If a sponsor fails to notify the beneficiary of its decision within the established time frames, the decision is deemed an automatic denial, at which point the sponsor must forward the case to the independent review entity, the second level of appeal.

Appeals

If a plan sponsor's coverage determination is unfavorable, it must provide the affected enrollee with a written denial notice that includes information on appeals rights. An appeal is a request for a further review of a coverage determination.[167] There are five levels of appeals.

Redetermination

The first level of appeal is a *redetermination* by the plan. An enrollee, enrollee's representative or enrollee's prescribing physician or other prescriber may request a standard or expedited redetermination by filing a written request with the plan sponsor. The request generally must be filed within 60 calendar days from the date printed or written on the written coverage determination denial notice. A Part D plan must also allow oral requests for standard redeterminations. If a physician asks for, or supports, an expedited appeal on the grounds that waiting seven days could seriously harm an enrollee's health, the appeal will automatically be expedited.[168]

Plan sponsors must provide immediate access to the redetermination process through their websites. CMS strongly encourages plans to establish interactive, web-based systems to meet this requirement.

A plan sponsor must also provide an enrollee or prescribing physician with a reasonable opportunity to present evidence, and the redetermination must be made by a person not involved in the original coverage decision.[169] Enrollees are to be notified of the results within seven days in the case of standard redetermination or within 72 hours for an expedited request.

Reconsideration by an Independent Review Entity

At the second level of appeal, an enrollee dissatisfied with a redetermination has a right to *reconsideration* by an independent review entity (IRE) working under contract with CMS, also known as a Qualified Independent Contractor (QIC). An enrollee or an enrollee's appointed representative may request a standard or expedited reconsideration. The request must be made within 60 days of a redetermination. The IRE is required to make a decision within seven days for a standard reconsideration and 72 hours for an expedited reconsideration.

According to CMS, Medicare handled 13,752 reconsideration cases in CY 2011, a reduction from 18,958 in 2010. In 54% of the 2011 cases, the plan sponsor's decision was overturned. Overall, 57% of the reconsiderations involved enrollee coverage determination requests for non-Part D drugs; 20% were for drug utilization management; 13% were off-formulary requests; 5% were cost-sharing disputes; 4% were for drug-tiering exceptions; and 1% involved out-of-network pharmacy coverage.[170]

Additional Levels of Appeal

If the above appeals result in decisions unfavorable to the enrollee, several additional levels of review may be pursued.

At the third level of appeal, an enrollee or the appointed representative may request a hearing with an *administrative law judge* (AUJ). A request must be made within 60 days of the IRE decision letter. To qualify for an AUJ hearing, the projected value of denied coverage must meet a minimum dollar amount ($140 in 2014). An enrollee cannot request an expedited hearing if the only issue at question involves a request for payment of Part D drugs that have already been furnished.[171] There is a 90-day limit for a regular decision and a 10-day limit for an expedited decision.

The fourth level of appeal is the *Medicare Appeals Council (MAC)*. A beneficiary or the appointed representative may request a review by the MAC within 60 days of the AUJ decision. The MAC may grant or deny the request for review. If it grants the request, it may issue a final decision or dismissal, or remand the case to the AUJ with instructions on how to proceed with the case. The review is to be completed within 90 days for a regular review and 10 days for an expedited review.

The final appeal level is a *federal district court*. A beneficiary or the appointed representative may request a review by a federal court within 60 days of the MAC decision notice. To receive a review by the court, the projected value of denied coverage must be greater than or equal to a minimum dollar amount ($1,430 in 2014).

Grievances

Grievances are complaints or disputes other than those involving coverage determinations. Grievances may include such things as complaints about a plan's customer service hours of operation, the time it takes to get a prescription filled, or a plan's benefit design. A grievance may also include a complaint that a Part D plan refused to expedite a coverage determination or redetermination. A beneficiary with a grievance may file a complaint within 60 days of the event. Although CMS regulations do not require a Part D plan sponsor to consider a grievance that is filed after the 60-day deadline, the regulations do not prevent a plan sponsor from doing so on a case-by-case basis.[172]

Plan sponsors must respond in a timely manner. A Part D plan sponsor must respond to an enrollee grievance within 24 hours if it involves a refusal by the Part D plan to grant an enrollee's request for an expedited coverage determination or an expedited redetermination and the enrollee has not yet purchased or received the drug in dispute.[173] (Sometimes a complaint may involve both a grievance and a coverage determination.)

Quality of Care Complaints

Complaints regarding quality of care received by Part D enrollees may be resolved by the plan sponsor, but also may be handled through a separate process: the Quality Improvement Organization (QIO) process.[174] The QIO program is implemented by a network of contractors throughout the United States that work with providers and beneficiaries to improve the quality of health care delivered to Medicare beneficiaries. When a Part D plan responds to an enrollee's grievance in writing, it must include a description of the enrollee's right to file a QIO grievance.[175] Quality of care grievances filed with a QIO may be filed and investigated beyond the 60-day time frame.

PROGRAM OVERSIGHT

The size, nature, and complexity of the Medicare Part D program put it at particular risk for fraud, waste, and abuse. The Part D program involves vulnerable beneficiaries, high-cost populations, and substantial control by plan sponsors. A variety of entities are involved in oversight activities to ensure program compliance and identify potentially fraudulent activities.

CMS Oversight

CMS is responsible for preventing and detecting fraud and abuse in Medicare Part D and ensuring sponsors' compliance with applicable requirements. CMS conducts a wide variety of oversight activities, such as bid reviews, marketing reviews, financial and accounting reviews, program audits, and UIS-readiness audits.[176] Some of the management controls used in the routine operation of Medicare Part D play a primary role in the administration of the benefit and a secondary role in fraud prevention and detection.

For each plan sponsor, CMS establishes a point of contact (account manager) for all communications with the plan. The account managers work with plans to resolve any problems, including compliance issues. As part of its oversight strategy, CMS conducts routine *program audits* to ensure compliance with various program requirements, including such things as enrollment and disenrollment, marketing and beneficiary information, pharmacy access, coordination of benefits, claims processing and payment, and grievances and coverage determinations.[177] CMS can also conduct separate, focused audits to confirm that a previously identified deficiency has been corrected or to check into an indication of non-compliance. These audits include a combination of desk and on-site activities.

In *financial audits*, CMS looks at the accuracy and validity of data reported by the plans. These audits, normally conducted after payment reconciliation, may examine things such as possible overpayments to plans, misrepresentation of bids, underreporting of rebates, and inaccurate prescription drug event data. If financial audits identify problems, CMS will recalculate payment reconciliation for that sponsor and target the sponsor for a future audit.

If egregious problems are identified, CMS actions can range from warning letters to civil monetary penalties or removal from the program, depending on the extent to which plans have violated Part D program requirements.

Oversight Responsibilities of Part D Sponsors

CMS requires plan sponsors to monitor and correct their own behavior, as well as the behavior of those they contract with. Part D sponsors are required by law to implement a comprehensive fraud and abuse program to detect, correct, and prevent fraud, waste, and abuse. Chapter 9 of CMS's *Prescription Drug Benefit Manual* provides both interpretive rules and guidelines for sponsors to follow in developing this program.[178]

Part D sponsors are required to have, and to implement, an effective compliance plan as a condition of participation in the Medicare program. Elements of an effective plan include written policies and procedures; a designated compliance officer and committee; training and education, effective lines of communication, well-publicized disciplinary guidelines, and internal monitoring and auditing; and prompt response to detected offences and development of corrective actions.

Part D sponsors are to provide fraud, waste, and abuse training and education to first-tier, downstream, and related entities.[179] This includes pharmacists, pharmacy clerks, and others who are employed by entities that plans contract with to provide the Medicare drug benefit. CMS also provides fraud awareness fact sheets that sponsors can send to beneficiaries.[180]

Medicare Prescription Drug Integrity Contractors

CMS contracts with a private firm, Health Integrity Inc.,[181] to act as the National Benefit Integrity Medicare Drug Integrity Contractor (NBI MEDIC) for Part D plans.[182] The NBI MEDIC's responsibilities include conducting complaint investigations; performing data analysis; developing and referring cases to law enforcement, as well as supporting ongoing investigations; conducting audits; reviewing PDP and MA-PD fraud and abuse compliance programs.

The NBI MEDIC is also responsible for working with other entities to coordinate fraud prevention and detection efforts, including the Part D sponsors, other Medicare contractors, the HHS Office of Inspector General (OIG), the Department of Justice, and state agencies.

Part D Recovery Audit Contractors

The ACA required CMS to expand its Recovery Audit Contractor (RAC) program to Medicare Part C and Part D. The law gave CMS authority contract with RACs to identify and reconcile overpayments and underpayments in Medicare Parts C and D. CMS has contracted with ACLR Strategic Business Solutions to perform the Part D RAC audit functions.[183]

Price Transparency

The Part D program relies on plan sponsors to generate prescription drug savings, in part, through their ability to negotiate price concessions such as rebates and discounts, with drug manufacturers and retail pharmacies. Sponsors must report the price concession amounts to CMS and pass some of these savings on to beneficiaries. CMS uses the reported data to calculate final plan payments; however, much of the information submitted to CMS is protected from disclosure.

In previous years, GAO has reported challenges in the oversight of federal prescription drug programs that rely on privately reported data.[184] Subsequent to that report, Section 6005 of the ACA required Part D plan sponsors and pharmacy benefit managers (PBM)[185] to report a variety of prescription drug pricing information to CMS.[186]

PROGRAM SPENDING AND FINANCING

Medicare's financial operations are accounted for through two trust funds maintained by the Department of the Treasury—the Hospital Insurance (HI) trust fund for Part A and the Supplementary Medical Insurance (SMI) trust fund, which contains separate accounts for Parts B and Part D.[187] Unlike the HI program, SMI was not intended to be fully supported through dedicated sources of income. Instead, it relies primarily on general tax revenues and beneficiary premiums as revenue sources.

Expenditures

According to the 2014 Medicare Trustees Report, during calendar year (CY) 2013, total Part D expenditures were approximately $69.7 billion.[188] (See **Table 11**.) This amount included the combined costs of prescription drugs provided by Part D plans to enrollees and Medicare payments to employer-sponsored retiree health plans ($69.3 billion). The remaining $0.4 billion in expenditures covered federal administrative expenses, including expenses incurred by the Department of Health and Human Services (HHS), the SSA, and the Department of the Treasury in administering Part D. Such duties include making payments to Part D plans and implementing fraud and abuse control activities. (See **Appendix** for historical and projected Part D expenditures.)

Revenues

The major sources of revenue for the Part D account include general revenues, beneficiary premiums, and state contributions. In CY2013, of the $69.7 billion in total Part D income, general revenues accounted for $51.0 billion (73.2%), premiums accounted for $9.9 billion (14.2%), and transfers from states for $8.8 billion (12.6%).

The appropriation language adopted for the Part D account provides resources for benefit payments without the need for congressional approval. This allows substantial flexibility in the amount of general revenues available to the account, and eliminates the need for a contingency reserve. As a result, assets in the Part D account are generally low and only need to be held for a short time until they are used to meet immediate expenditures. As premium and general revenue income for Part D is reset each year to match expected costs, the Medicare Trustees consider the Part D account to be in satisfactory financial condition under current law.

Beneficiary Premiums

Beneficiary premiums are based on the participating plans' national average bid amounts and are defined prior to each year's operations,[189] with the average premium amounting to 25.5% of the expected per capita plan costs for basic coverage. (See "Premiums.") In 2014, the base monthly premium is $32.42, however beneficiaries pay different premiums depending on the plan they have selected (and whether they are entitled to low-income premium subsidies). Beneficiaries may have their premiums deducted from their Social Security or other federal benefit payments; these are then forwarded to Part D plans on their behalf. Alternatively, they may pay their premiums directly to the Part D plans.

As required by ACA, beginning in 2011, beneficiaries with higher incomes pay income-adjusted premiums in addition to the premiums charged by the plans in which they have enrolled.[190] These extra amounts are credited to the Part D trust fund account and reduce the amount of general revenue funding needed. Because individual plan premiums vary, the additional amount paid is calculated as a percentage of the base beneficiary premium, not the individual's actual premium amount. This extra amount is usually deducted from an individual's monthly Social Security payments regardless of how that person ordinarily pays the monthly prescription plan premiums. If the amount is greater than the monthly payment from Social Security, or an individual does not receive Social Security payments (e.g., the individual has not yet signed up for Social Security benefits), then the Centers for Medicare & Medicaid Services (CMS) may directly bill the individual for this amount.

In 2013, $3.2 billion in premium amounts were withheld from Social Security benefit checks or other federal benefit payments. Another $6.7 billion in premiums were paid directly to the plans by beneficiaries. As noted, premiums for the Part D program are generally set at an amount equal to 25.5% of standard benefit costs; however, as recipients of the Part D low-income subsidies are not required to pay premiums and premiums are based only on standard benefits (e.g., the premium calculation does not include such things as costs associated with the low-income subsidy and risk-corridor payments), premiums covered about 14% of total Part D program costs in 2013.

General Revenues

General revenues are transferred from the Treasury to the Part D Account on an as-needed basis to cover the portion of program expenditures funded by federal subsidies. These transfers are based on expected costs of the direct subsidy, reinsurance payments, employer subsidies, low- income subsidies, net risk-sharing payments, administrative expenses, and advanced discount payments.[191]

In CY2013, contributions received from the general fund of the Treasury amounted to $51.0 billion, or about 73% of total Part D revenue.

State Contributions

Subsequent to the availability of Part D drug coverage and low-income subsidies in 2006, Medicaid is no longer the primary payer of drug costs for full-benefit dual-eligible beneficiaries.

Table 11. Statement of Operations of Part D Account, CY2013 (in millions)

Assets at Beginning of Year	**$999.9**
Revenues	$69,670.6
Premiums from Enrollees	9,928.6
Premiums deducted from Social Security checks	*3,208.7*
Premiums paid directly to plans	*6,719.9*
Government Contributions	50,958.2
Prescription drug benefits	*50,586.6*
Administrative expenses	*371.6*
Payments from States	8,775.8
Revenues	$69,670.6
Interest on Investments	8.0
Expenditures	$69,677.4
Benefit Payments	69,305.8
Federal Administrative Expenses	371.6
Assets at End of Year	$993.0

Source: 2014 Annual Report of the Boards of Trustees of the Federal Hospital Insurance and Federal Supplementary Insurance Trust Funds, July 28, 2014, Table III.D1.

Note: Totals may not add due to rounding.

However, MMA contained a provision (labeled by some as the "clawback provision") that requires states to pay the Part D account in the SMI trust fund a portion of the costs that they would have incurred for this population if they were still the primary payer. These amounts are based on the product of the estimated annual per capita full dual-eligible drug payment amount and the monthly State enrollment of full dual eligibles. Starting in 2006, states paid 90% of these estimated costs. This percentage phases down over a 10-year period to 75% in 2015. In 2013, state payments amounted to $8.8 billion, or about 13% of Part D revenues.[192]

Historical Program Spending

Actual spending for the Medicare prescription drug benefit has been lower than estimated at the beginning of the program. The 2004 Medicare Trustees Report, the first of such reports issued subsequent to the enactment of MMA, projected that total program spending would be $85 billion in 2006 (the first year of the program) and would grow to $162 billion by 2013. Actual Medicare expenditures for the Part D drug benefit were approximately $47 billion in 2006 and close to $70 billion in 2013. The difference between projected and actual spending has been due to both lower than expected enrollment and per capita spending. (See **Table 12.**) Original CBO estimates of Part D spending were also higher than actual spending for FY2004-FY2013.

While aggregate Part D expenditures have increased by an average annual rate of 5.7% over the past seven years, most of this growth reflects the rapid growth in enrollment during the initial years of the program. Per capita expenditures during this time increased at a much slower rate annual rate of 0.5%. Both the Medicare Trustees and the Congressional Budget Office (CBO) attribute the slower per capita growth rate to a high proportion of prescriptions filled with low- cost generic drugs, as well as to patent expirations of major drugs during this period.[193] (See **Table 13.**)

Estimated Future Part D Expenditures

During the next 10 years, the 2014 Medicare Trustees Report projects that total Part D expenditures will reach $172 billion in 2023. Per capita benefits are projected to increase from $1,901 in 2013 to $3,206 in 2023.

As noted, average annual growth for Part D over the past seven years has been around 5.7%, with most of this growth due to increased enrollment rather than increased per capita spending. However, the Trustees project more rapid cost growth over the next 10 years, with aggregate benefits increasing, on average, at 9.5% annually and per capita expenditures increasing at 6.0% each year, due to expectations of further increases in the number of enrollees, costs associated with the gradual elimination of the coverage gap, changes in the distribution of enrollees among coverage categories (e.g., a movement from subsidized retiree plans to regular Part D plans), a slowing of the trend toward greater generic drug utilization, and an increase in the use and the prices of specialty drugs. Over the longer term, the Trustees project total Part D spending will grow from 0.44% of GDP in 2013, to 1.36% of GDP in 2085.

Table 12. Comparison of Projected and Actual Part D Enrollment and Spending Calendar Years 2006-2013

	Enrollment (in thousands)		**Per Enrollee Spending**		**Total Part D Spending (in billions)**	
	2004 Trustees Report (Projected)[a]	**2014 Trustees Report** (Actual)[b]	**2004 Trustees Report** (Projected)	**2014 Trustees Report** (Actual)	**2004 Trustees Report** (Projected)	**2014 Trustees Report** (Actual)
2006	40.736	30,560	$1,733	$1,619	$85.0	$47.4
2007	41,468	31,392	1,861	1,630	93.0	49.7
2008	42,296	32,589	1,999	1,662	101.9	49.3
2009	43,158	33,644	2,139	1,730	111.2	60.8
2010	44,069	34,772	2,279	1,808	120.9	62.1
2011	45,117	35,720	2,419	1,859	131.4	67.1
2012	46,374	37,402	2,615	1,847	145.6	66.9
2013	47,761	39,095	2,820	1,901	161.8	69.7

Source: CRS analysis of data from the 2004 and 2014 Reports of the Medicare Trustees.

Notes:

[a] All data from the 2004 report are projected.

[b] All data from the 2014 report reflect actual spending.

Table 13. Comparison of Original CBO Estimates and Actual Part D Costs, FY2004-FY2013
($ in billions)

		2004	**2005**	**2006**	**2007**	**2008**	**2009**	**2010**	**2011**	**2012**	**2013**	**2004-2013**	**% Actual Different from Projected**
Federal Spending	CBO Original Cost Estimate	$0.6	$1.5	$32.1	$52.9	$59.9	$65.7	$72.6	$79.5	$88.5	$98.9	$552.2	
	2014 Medicare Trustees Report[a]	0.2	1.2	27.7	41.5	35.4	43.5	52.7	57.0	44.4	50.1	353.7	**35.9% less**
Total Spending	CBO Original Cost Estimate	0.6	1.5	46.8	74.8	84.2	92.0	101.3	110.6	122.8	136.8	771.4	
	2014 Medicare Trustees Report[a]	0.2	1.2	33.9	52.4	47.2	56.8	63.8	71.0	60.9	68.3	455.7	**40.9% less**

Source: Congressional Budget Office, Projection of Spending for the Medicare Part D Benefit: Letter to the Honorable William "Bill" M. Thomas, February 9, 2005; and the 2014 Medicare Trustees Report, July 28, 2014, Table V.H8.

[a] The figures in this table are for fiscal years, while those in **Table 11** are for calendar years.

[b] Actual federal Medicare Part D cost is measured as total expenditures less premium income and transfers from states. Trustee report figures for FY2004-FY2013 reflect actual spending.

APPENDIX. HISTORICAL AND PROJECTED PART D OPERATIONS

Table A-1. Operation of the Part D Account in the SMI Trust Fund, Calendar Years 2004-2023 ($ in billions)

Income					Expenditures			Trust Fund	
Year	Premiums	General Revenue	Transfers from States	Total	Benefit Payments	Admin. Expenses	Total	Net Change	Balance at End of Year
Historical Data									
2004	—	$0.4	—	$0.4	$0.4	—	$0.4	—	—
2005	—	1.1	—	1.1	1.1	—	1.1	0	0
2006	$3.5	39.2	$5.5	48.2	47.1	$0.3	47.4	$0.8	$0.8
2007	4.1	38.8	6.9	49.7	48.8	0.9	49.7	0.0	0.8
2008	5.0	37.3	7.1	49.4	49.0	0.3	49.3	0.1	0.9
2009	6.3	47.1	7.6	61.0	60.5	0.3	60.8	0.1	1.1
2010	6.5	51.1	4.0	61.7	61.7	0.4	62.1	-0.4	0.7
2011	7.7	52.6	7.1	67.4	66.7	0.4	67.1	0.3	1.0
2012	8.3	50.1	8.4	66.9	66.5	0.4	66.9	0.0	1.0
2013	9.9	51.0	8.8	69.7	69.3	0.4	69.7	0.0	1.0
Intermediate Estimates									
2014	11.6	59.2	8.3	79.1	79.0	0.4	79.4	−0.3	0.7
2015	13.6	64.5	8.5	86.7	86.3	0.4	86.7	0.0	0.7
2016	15.4	70.0	9.1	94.5	94.0	0.4	94.5	0.1	0.8
2017	17.7	75.2	9.8	102.6	102.1	0.4	102.6	0.1	0.8
2018	19.6	81.8	10.6	112.0	111.4	0.5	111.9	0.1	0.9
2019	21.7	89.2	11.5	122.4	121.9	0.5	122.3	0.1	1.0

Table A-1. (Continued)

Income					Expenditures			Trust Fund	
Year	Premiums	General Revenue	Transfers from States	Total	Benefit Payments	Admin. Expenses	Total	Net Change	Balance at End of Year
2020	23.8	97.9	12.5	134.1	133.5	0.5	134.0	0.1	1.1
2021	25.3	106.7	13.5	145.5	144.9	0.5	145.4	0.1	1.1
2022	28.0	115.5	14.7	158.3	157.6	0.5	158.2	0.1	1.2
2023	30.6	125.2	16.0	171.8	171.2	0.6	171.7	0.1	1.4

Source: 2014 Medicare Trustees Report, Table III.D3.

Notes: Sums may not equal totals due to rounding. Some of the fluctuation in year by year spending is due to the payment structure of the Part D program. For example, in 2006, plan bids and therefore payments were higher than actual spending; the $4 billion in reconciliation payments resulted in lower per capita Part D spending in 2007 and 2008. On the other hand, in 2008 spending exceeded plan bids, and therefore more than $2 billion was added to 2009 outlays. The Medicare Trustees expect that in 2013, spending will exceed plan bids by about $6 billion, and reconciliation payments in that amount will need to be paid to Part D plans in 2014.

End Notes

[1] The regulations governing the Part D program are set forth in 42 C.F.R. Part 423—Voluntary Medicare Prescription Drug Benefit. The Part D program has also been modified by the QI, TMA, and Abstinence Programs Extension and Hurricane Katrina Unemployment Relief Act of 2005 (P.L. 109-91); the Tax Relief and Health Care Act of 2006 (TRHCA, P.L. 109-432); and the Medicare Improvements for Patients and Providers Act of 2008 (MIPPA, P.L. 110- 275).

[2] CMS, "Monthly Contract Summary Report," September 2014, http://www.cms.gov/Research-Statistics-Data-and-Systems/Statistics-Trends-and-Reports/MCRAdvPartDEnrolData /Monthly-Contract-and-Enrollment-Summary-Report-Items/Contract-Summary-2014-09.html?DLPage=1&DLSort=1&DLSortDir=descending. The 2014 enrollment is an increase from 36.2 million in December, 2013, http://www.cms.gov/Research-Statistics-Data-and-Systems/Statistics-Trends-and-Reports/MCRAdvPartDEnrolData/Monthly-Contract-and-Enrollment-Summary-Report-Items/Contract-Summary-2013-12.html?DLPage=1&DLSort=1&DLSortDir=descending.

[3] The 2014 Annual Report of the Boards of Trustees of the Federal Hospital Insurance and Federal Supplementary Medical Insurance Trust Funds, Table IV.B7, http://www.cms.gov /Research-Statistics-Data-and-Systems/Statistics-Trends-and-Reports/ReportsTrustFunds /downloads/tr2014.pdf. The trustees estimate that the number of LIS beneficiaries will remain about the same in 2014.

[4] The coverage gap refers to the period when a Medicare beneficiary has exceeded a drug plan's standard payment threshold and faces higher out-of-pocket expenses until he or she reaches a "catastrophic limit." Once the catastrophic limit is reached, federal subsidies cover most prescription costs.

[5] MedPAC, *Report to the Congress, Medicare Payment Policy*, March 2014, p. 369, http://www.medpac.gov/chapters/ Mar14_Ch14.pdf.

[6] CMS in 2014 proposed that, in order to be eligible for Medicare prescription drug benefits, an enrollee must be a U.S. citizen or qualified alien who is lawfully present in the United States. CMS, "Medicare Program; Contract Year 2015 Policy and Technical Changes to the Medicare Advantage and the Medicare Prescription Drug Benefit Programs; Proposed Rule," 79 *Federal Register*, p. 1932, January 10, 2014, http://www.gpo.gov/fdsys/pkg/FR-2014-01-10/pdf/ 2013-31497.pdf. CMS has not finalized the proposed rule.

[7] The Medicare Savings program includes the Qualified Medicare Beneficiary program (QMB), Specified Low-Income Medicare Beneficiary program (SLMB), and Qualifying Individual program (QI). These programs help Medicare beneficiaries of modest means pay all or some of Medicare's cost-sharing amounts (i.e., premiums, deductibles, and copayments). To qualify, an individual must be eligible for Medicare and must meet certain income limits which change annually.

[8] Supplemental Security Income (SSI) is a federal income supplement program funded by general tax revenues (not Social Security taxes). It is designed to help aged, blind, and disabled people who have little or no income, and it provides cash to meet basic needs for food, clothing, and shelter.

[9] Social Security benefits, veterans' benefits, public and private pensions, annuities, and in-kind support are counted as income. The 2014 income limits apply for LIS beneficiaries who seek benefits after January 1, 2014. HHS sets separate poverty levels for Alaska and Hawaii. Resource limits include a $1,500 burial allowance. See SSA Program Operations Manual, "HI 03001.020 Eligibility for Extra Help (Prescription Drug Low-Income

Subsidy)," https://secure.ssa.gov/ poms.nsf/lnx/0603001020#c3; and SSA,"HI 03001.005 Medicare Part D Extra Help (Low-Income Subsidy or LIS)," https://secure.ssa.gov /poms.nsf/lnx/0603001005.

[10] Income and asset tests may vary by state and change each year.

[11] CMS, "2013 Reassignment." Excel file at http://www.cms.gov/Medicare/Eligibility-and-Enrollment/ LowIncSubMedicarePresCov/Reassignment.html; and CRS Report R41196, *Medicare Provisions in the Patient Protection and Affordable Care Act (PPACA): Summary and Timeline*, coordinated by Patricia A. Davis.

[12] CMS, "2013 Reassignment for January 2014." Available at http://www.cms.gov/Medicare /Eligibility-and- Enrollment/LowIncSubMedicarePresCov/Reassignment.html.

[13] SSA, "HI 03030.025, Resource Limits for Subsidy Eligibility," https://secure.ssa.gov/poms.nsf /lnx/0603030025.

[14] CMS, *Medicare Part D Prescription Drug Manual*, Chapter 13, "Premium and Cost-Sharing Subsidies for Low- Income Individuals," Rev. July 29, 2011, www.cms.gov/Regulations-and- Guidance/Guidance/Transmittals/Downloads/Chapter13.pdf.

[15] CMCS Informational Bulletin, "Annual Redetermination of Medicare Part D Low-Income Subsidy Deemed Status (Re-deeming)," June 14, 2013, http://www.medicaid.gov/Federal-Policy-Guidance/downloads/CIB-06-14-2013.pdf.

[16] The extension is for one year from the date upon which the couple's next scheduled redetermination would have occurred. CMS, *Medicare Part D Prescription Drug Manual*, Chapter 13, "Premium and Cost-Sharing Subsidies for Low-Income Individuals," Section 40.1.3, Rev. July 29, 2011, http://www.cms.gov/Regulations-and- Guidance/Guidance /Transmittals/Downloads/Chapter13.pdf.

[17] CMS, "Understanding Medicare Part C & D Enrollment Periods," http://www.medicare.gov /Pubs/pdf/11219.pdf.

[18] CMS, *Medicare & You*, Section 6, http://www.medicare.gov/pubs/pdf/10050.pdf.

[19] See CRS Report R40082, *Medicare: Part B Premiums*, by Patricia A. Davis.

[20] Shinobu Suzuki, MedPAC, "Medicare Part D's Competitive Design: Do Part D Enrollees Switch Plans?" June 23, 2013, http://academyhealth.org/files/2013/sunday/suzuki.pdf.

[21] This includes being released from jail or out of an institution.

[22] CMS, "Understanding Medicare Part C & D Enrollment Periods," http://www.medicare.gov /Pubs/pdf/11219.pdf. The publication includes other examples of SEPs.

[23] The late enrollment penalty is calculated based on the national base beneficiary premium, not the plan's premium. Therefore, the penalty is billed to applicable enrollees even if the plan's Part D basic premium is $0.

[24] CMS, "What's the Part D Late Enrollment Penalty?," http://www.medicare.gov/part-d/costs/penalty/part-d-late- enrollment-penalty.html. (To calculate, 1% x 30 months equals .30. $32.42 x .30 equals $9.73. The amount is then rounded to $9.70.)

[25] CMS, Open Enrollment Center, http://www.cms.gov/Center/Special-Topic/Open-Enrollment-Center.html.

[26] Medicare Plan Finder, http://www.medicare.gov/find-a-plan/questions/home.aspx.

[27] For example, a plan with the lowest premium and/or no deductible may end up not being the lowest cost plan for the beneficiary if the costs for the beneficiary's drugs are more than under a different plan.

[28] The plans are rated on how well they perform in different categories, including (1) drug plan customer service, (e.g., how long members wait on hold and how frequently they meet deadlines for timely appeals); (2) member complaints and number of beneficiaries staying with the same drug plan; (3) member satisfaction with drug plans; and (4) drug pricing and patient safety, including how often drug plans update their prices and formulary information

on the Medicare website and how similar a drug plan's estimated prices on the Medicare website are to prices members pay at the pharmacy. The ratings range from one to five stars, with one star meaning "poor" and five starts meaning "excellent."

[29] SHIPs are state-based programs that use community-based networks to provide Medicare beneficiaries with local personalized assistance on a wide variety of Medicare and health insurance topics and receive federal funding for their activities. See http://www.medicare.gov/contacts.

[30] Medicare.gov, "5-Star Special Enrollment Period," http://www.medicare.gov/sign-up-change-plans/when-can-i-join-a-health-or-drug-plan/five-star-enrollment/5-star-enrollment-period. html.

[31] CMS, *Medicare Prescription Drug Benefit Manual*, Chapter 2, "2014 Medicare Marketing Guidelines," Section 30.10, Rev. June 28, 2013, available at http://www.cms.gov /Medicare/Prescription-Drug-Coverage/ PrescriptionDrugCovContra/PartDManuals.html.

[32] CMS, "Medicare Program; Changes to the Medicare Advantage and the Medicare Prescription Drug Benefit Programs for Contract Year 2013 and Other Changes; Final Rule," 77 *Federal Register*, April 12, 2012, http://www.gpo.gov/fdsys/pkg/FR-2012-04-12/pdf/2012-8071.pdf.

[33] CMS, "Suspension of Termination of Low Performing Icon (LPI) Plans for 2015," September 8, 2014, http://op.bna.com/hl.nsf/id/myon-9ntnrm/$File/terminatema.pdf.

[34] CMS, "5-Star Plan Ratings," http://www.cms.gov/Outreach-and-Education/Training/CMS NationalTrainingProgram/ Downloads/2013-5-Star-Enrollment-Period-Job-Aid.pdf.

[35] CMS, *Medicare Prescription Drug Benefit Manual*, Chapter 2, "2014 Medicare Marketing Guidelines," Rev. June 28, 2013, available at http://www.cms.gov/Medicare/Prescription-Drug-Coverage/PrescriptionDrugCovContra/ PartDManuals.html.

[36] CMS, *Medicare Prescription Drug Benefit Manual*, Chapter 2, "2014 Medicare Marketing Guidelines," Rev. June 28, 2013, available at http://www.cms.gov/Medicare/Prescription-Drug-Coverage/PrescriptionDrugCovContra/ PartDManuals.html.

[37] CMS, *Medicare Prescription Drug Benefit Manual*, Chapter 3, "Eligibility, Enrollment and Disenrollment," Rev. August 30, 2013, http://www.cms.gov/Medicare/Eligibility-and-Enrollment/MedicarePresDrugEligEnrol/Downloads/ CY-2014-PDP-Enrollment-and-Disenrollment-Guidance-r.pdf.

[38] Medicare drug plan participation in Medicare's enrollment center is voluntary, so not all Medicare drug plans will offer this option.

[39] CMS, *Medicare Prescription Drug Benefit Manual*, Chapter 3, "Eligibility, Enrollment and Disenrollment," Rev. August 30, 2013, http://www.cms.gov/Medicare/Eligibility-and-Enrollment/MedicarePresDrugEligEnrol/Downloads/CY-2014-PDP-Enrollment-and-Disenrollment-Guidance-r.pdf.

[40] Full-benefit duals who live in another country, live in one of the five U.S. territories, are inmates in a correctional facility, have already enrolled in a Part D plan, or have opted out of auto-enrollment into a Part D plan are excepted from this process.

[41] CMS, "2013 Reassignment," Excel file at http://www.cms.gov/Medicare/Eligibility-and-Enrollment/ LowIncSubMedicarePresCov/Reassignment.html.

[42] CMS, *Medicare Prescription Drug Benefit Manual*, Chapter 3, "Eligibility, Enrollment and Disenrollment," Rev. August 30, 2013, Section 40.1.5, http://www.cms.gov /Medicare/Eligibility-and-Enrollment/ MedicarePresDrugEligEnrol/Downloads/CY-2014-PDP-Enrollment-and-Disenrollment-Guidance-r.pdf.

[43] CMS, "Annual Release of Part D National Average Bid Amount and other C & D Bid Related Information," July 30, 2013, http://www.cms.gov/Medicare/Health-Plans/MedicareAdvtg SpecRateStats/downloads/ PartDandMAbenchmarks2014.pdf.

[44] Medicare Advantage plans are required to use 75% of the difference between the plan's benchmark payment and its bid for providing required Part A and Part B services (called the *Part C rebate*) to supplement its package of benefits or lower its premium. Many MA plans use some of their rebate dollars to enhance their Part D benefit or to reduce the portion of their plan premium associated with drug coverage.

[45] Social Security deductions are limited to $300 per month, the "harm limit." Social Security Administration, "Withholding Medicare Prescription Drug Premium from Your 2014 Social Security Payment," http://www.medicare.gov/pubs/pdf/11400.pdf.

[46] CRS Report R40082, *Medicare: Part B Premiums*, by Patricia A. Davis.

[47] The definition of modified adjusted gross income used for the calculation is the total of adjusted gross income and tax-exempt interest income. The income data is based on the most recent tax information that the Internal Revenue Service is able to provide the SSA. Generally, the tax information is from two years prior to the year for which the premium is being determined, but not more than three years prior. Social Security Administration, *Medicare Premiums: Rules for Higher-Income Beneficiaries*, 2014, http://www.ssa.gov /pubs/EN-05-10536.pdf. MAGI has more than one definition in federal tax law, with the definition varying based on the program or provision utilizing the concept.

[48] The thresholds are the same as those used for calculating Medicare Part B premiums.

[49] Social Security Administration, *Medicare Premiums: Rules for Higher-Income Beneficiaries*, 2014, http://www.ssa.gov/pubs/EN-05-10536.pdf.

[50] CMS, "Annual Release of Part D National Average Bid Amount and other C & D Bid Related Information," July 30, 2013, http://www.cms.gov/Medicare/Health-Plans/MedicareAdvtg SpecRateStats/downloads/ PartDandMAbenchmarks2014.pdf.

[51] Social Security Administration, *Medicare Premiums: Rules for Higher-Income Beneficiaries*, 2014, http://www.ssa.gov/pubs/EN-05-10536.pdf.

[52] In cases where an enrollee's benefit payment check is not sufficient to have the IRMMA withheld, or if an enrollee is not receiving such benefits, the beneficiary must be billed directly for the IRMMA. 42 C.F.R. §423.293.

[53] Social Security Act, §1860D-2.

[54] CMS, "2013 Medicare Part D Landscape," p. 15, September 19, 2012. Link to document can be found at 2013 Landscape Presentations at http://www.cms.gov/Medicare/Prescription-Drug-Coverage/PrescriptionDrugCovGenIn/ index.html?redirect=/PrescriptionDrugCovGenIn/. Actuarially equivalent standard coverage can include plans that reduce cost-sharing to $0 for generic or preferred Part D drugs, as long as the overall cost-sharing structure is actuarially equivalent to 25% co-insurance for costs above the annual deductible and up to the initial coverage limit and/or to average expected cost-sharing in the catastrophic portion of the benefit. See CMS, *Medicare Prescription Drug Benefit Manual*, Chapter 5, "Benefits and Beneficiary Protection," Section 20, September 20, 2011, http://www.cms.gov/Medicare/Prescription-Drug-Coverage/PrescriptionDrugCovContra/Downloads/MemoPDBManualChapter5_093011. pdf.

[55] CMS, *Medicare Prescription Drug Benefit Manual*, Chapter 5, "Benefits and Beneficiary Protection," Section 20.4.4, September 20, 2011, http://www.cms.gov/Medicare /Prescription-Drug-Coverage/PrescriptionDrugCovContra/Downloads/MemoPDB Manual Chapter5_093011.pdf.

[56] There are actually two catastrophic thresholds. One is for individuals receiving a low-income subsidy who are not eligible for manufacturer discounts in the doughnut hole. Their

threshold is about $6,455. For beneficiaries eligible for the manufacturer discount, the threshold is about $6,690.77.

[57] Total reflects catastrophic limit of about $6,690.77 minus initial coverage limit of $2,850. Actual spending per beneficiary will vary depending on plan design and purchases of brand-name vs. generic drugs. CMS thresholds are based on average spending data across all plans.

[58] Nominal cost sharing is defined as the greater of (1) a copayment of $2.55 in 2014 for a generic drug or preferred multiple source drug and $6.35 in 2014 for other drugs, or (2) 5% coinsurance.

[59] Social Security Act, §1860D-2.

[60] MedPAC, *Health Care Spending and the Medicare Program*, chart 10-5, June 2014, http://www.medpac.gov/ documents/Jun14DataBookEntireReport.pdf.

[61] CMS, *Medicare Prescription Drug Benefit Manual*, Chapter 5, "Benefits and Beneficiary Protection," September 20, 2011, http://www.cms.gov/Medicare/Prescription-Drug-Coverage/PrescriptionDrugCovContra/Downloads/MemoPDBManualChapter5_093011.pdf.

[62] CMS, "Plan and Beneficiary Characteristics Associated with the Coverage Gap and Catastrophic Phase," Presentation to Medicare Part D Conference, 2012. Link can be found at http://www.cms.gov/Outreach-and-Education/ Training/CTEO/Event_Archives.html#%20CMS%202012%20Medicare%20Advantage%20&%20Prescription%20Drug%20Plan%20Fall%20Enrollment,%20Marketing,%20&%20Compliance%20Conference.

[63] MedPAC, *Health Care Spending and the Medicare Program*, June 2014, Charts 10-5 and 10-6, http://www.medpac.gov/documents/Jun14DataBookEntireReport.pdf.

[64] For more information on the coverage gap see CMS, "Bridging the Coverage Gap," at http://www.cms.gov/ Medicare/Prescription-Drug-Coverage/PrescriptionDrugCovGenIn/bridgingthegap.html; CMS, "Costs in the Coverage Gap," at http://www.medicare.gov/part-d/costs/coverage-gap/part-d-coverage-gap.html; and CMS, "Medicare Prescription Drug Coverage, Closing the Coverage Gap—Medicare Prescription Drugs Are Becoming More Affordable," at http://www.medicare.gov/Pubs/pdf/11493.pdf.

[65] Part D sponsors are required to ensure that their network pharmacies inform enrollees of any price differential between a covered drug and the lowest-price generic version of the drug that is therapeutically equivalent, bioequivalent, on the plan's formulary, and available at that pharmacy.

[66] Some states offer payment assistance for drug plan premiums and/or other drug costs for individuals who have trouble affording their medication but do not qualify for LIS. For example, a state may offer assistance to individuals with incomes between 150% and 300% of the FPL. To learn which states offer this assistance and for details on the state programs, see http://www.medicare.gov/pharmaceutical-assistance-program/state-programs.aspx.

[67] Many major drug manufacturers offer assistance programs for the drugs they manufacture. The value of benefits received under these programs does not count toward true out-of-pocket expenses. To learn which manufacturers offer assistance, see http://www.medicare.gov/pharmaceutical-assistance-program/index.aspx.

[68] CMS, "Part D Information for Pharmaceutical Manufacturers," http://www.cms.gov/Medicare/Prescription-Drug- Coverage/PrescriptionDrugCovGenIn/Pharma.html.

[69] CMS, "Medicare Prescription Drug Coverage, Closing the Coverage Gap—Medicare Prescription Drugs Are Becoming More Affordable," p. 4, http://www.medicare.gov/Pubs/pdf/11493.pdf.

[70] CMS, "Coverage Gap Discount Program," http://www.cms.gov/Medicare/Medicare-Advantage/Plan-Payment/CGDP.html. Companies that make brand-name prescription drugs that want to participate in Part D must sign agreements with CMS to participate in the Medicare Coverage Gap Discount Program.

[71] CBO, "Offsetting Effects of Prescription Drug Use on Medicare's Spending for Medical Services," November 2012, p. 6, http://www.cbo.gov/sites/default /files/cbofiles /attachments/43741-MedicalOffsets-11-29-12.pdf. CBO estimates that the manufacturer discounts and increased government drug coverage will increase federal spending for Medicare Part D by $86 billion from 2013–2022, compared to what would have been spent under prior law. CBO also estimates that closing the coverage gap will reduce federal spending for medical services under Medicare by $35 billion, resulting in a net increase in federal spending of $51 billion from 2013 to 2022.

[72] True out-of-pocket costs are the payments that count toward an enrollee's Part D out-of-pocket threshold of $4,550 for 2014. Full-subsidy eligible beneficiaries have no deductible and minimal cost sharing in the initial coverage period and coverage gap.

[73] CMS, "Understanding True-Out-of-Pocket (TrOOP) Costs," http://www.cms.gov/Outreach-and-Education/Outreach/ Partnerships/downloads/11223-P.pdf.

[74] Added by §3314 of the ACA.

[75] Added by §3314 of the ACA.

[76] For brand-name drugs, any pharmacy dispensing fees are added to the price of the drug after the manufacturer's discount has been applied, and the full amount of the fee counts as TrOOP. For generic drugs, dispensing fees are counted as part of the cost of the drug before the government subsidy is applied. Therefore, only a percentage of the dispending fee, not the full amount, is counted in TrOOP.

[77] Examples are from CMS, "Medicare Prescription Drug Coverage, Closing the Coverage Gap—Medicare Prescription Drugs Are Becoming More Affordable," http://www.medicare.gov/Pubs/pdf/11493.pdf.

[78] A full-benefit dual eligible is someone who is qualified for full Medicaid benefits. Full-benefit beneficiaries may be deemed full-subsidy Medicare Part D recipients if they meet certain guidelines. See CMS, *Medicare Part D Prescription Drug Manual*, Chapter 13, "Premium and Cost-Sharing Subsidies for Low-Income Individuals," p. 5, July 29, 2011, available at http://www.cms.gov/Medicare/Prescription-Drug-Coverage/PrescriptionDrugCovContra/ PartDManuals.html.

[79] CMS, *Medicare Part D Prescription Drug Manual*, Chapter 13, "Premium and Cost-Sharing Subsidies for Low- Income Individuals," Section 60.2.1., July 29, 2011. Available at http://www.cms.gov/Medicare/Prescription-Drug-Coverage/PrescriptionDrugCovContra/PartDManuals.html.

[80] CMS, "Retiree Drug Subsidy," http://rds.cms.hhs.gov/.

[81] CMS, "2014 Final Call Letter," p. 59, http://www.cms.gov/Medicare/Health-Plans/Medicare AdvtgSpecRateStats/ downloads/Announcement2014.pdf.

[82] Internal Revenue Service, "Frequently Asked Questions: Retiree Drug Subsidy," http://www.irs.gov/uac/Newsroom/ Frequently-Asked-Questions:-Retiree-Drug-Subsidy.

[83] 2014 Annual Report of the Boards of Trustees of the Federal Hospital Insurance and Federal Supplementary Medical Insurance Trust Funds, p. 148, http://www.cms.gov/Research-Statistics-Data-and-Systems/Statistics-Trends-and-Reports/ReportsTrustFunds/downloads/tr2014.pdf.

[84] This approach may have some financial consequences for the employer or union since third-party payments do not count toward TrOOP. Thus, if an employer chooses to pay some of

the Part D cost sharing on behalf of its retirees, this would have the effect of delaying the point at which the Part D catastrophic coverage would begin.

[85] CMS, *Medicare Prescription Drug Benefit Manual*, Chapter 12, Rev. November 7, 2008, http://www.cms.gov/Regulations-and-Guidance/Guidance/Transmittals/Downloads /R6PDB.pdf.

[86] Ibid, Sections 20.10 and 20.11.

[87] 2014 Annual Report of the Boards of Trustees of the Federal Hospital Insurance and Federal Supplementary Medical Insurance Trust Funds, p. 148, http://www.cms.gov/Research-Statistics-Data-and-Systems/Statistics-Trends-and-Reports/ReportsTrustFunds/downloads/tr2014.pdf.

[88] These changes were required by Section 175 of the Medicare Improvements for Patients and Providers Act (MIPPA, P.L. 110-275).

[89] CMS, "2014 Final Call Letter," April 1, 2013, pp. 152-153, http://www.cms.gov /Medicare/Health-Plans/ MedicareAdvtgSpecRateStats/downloads/Announcement2014.pdf.

[90] The committee may be set up by a sponsor or a pharmacy benefit manager acting on behalf of the plan sponsor. Committee members must sign conflict of interest statements detailing economic or other relationships with entities affected by drug coverage decisions that could influence committee decisions.

[91] The United States Pharmacopeial Convention (USP) is a nonprofit organization that sets standards for the identity, strength, quality, and purity of medicines, food ingredients and dietary supplements.

[92] CMS, *Medicare Prescription Drug Benefit Manual,* Chapter 6, "Part D Drugs and Formulary Requirements," Rev. February 19, 2010, http://www.cms.gov/Medicare/Prescription-Drug-Coverage/PrescriptionDrugCovContra/ Downloads/Chapter6.pdf.

[93] For beneficiaries beginning treatment in these categories, such management techniques may be used for categories other than HIV/AIDS drugs.

[94] Monica Reed, "Part D Protected Drug Class," CMS 2012 Prescription Drug Benefit Symposium, http://origin- qps.onstreammedia.com/origin/providerre/CMS/Media/1203 Baltimore/transcripts/ d1_02_PartDProtectedDrugClass_Reed.pdf.

[95] Ibid.

[96] In January 2014, CMS issued proposed rules that would have narrowed the protected classes to anticonvulsants, antiretrovirals, and antineoplastics, beginning in plan year 2015. Antipsychotic drugs would have continued to be treated as a class of clinical concern in 2015 and until CMS determined that it was appropriate to change the criteria for these products. In May 2014, CMS announced it would not finalize the proposed regulations relating to the six protected classes. See CMS, "Medicare Program; Contract Year 2015 Policy and Technical Changes to the Medicare Advantage and the Medicare Prescription Drug Benefit Programs; Proposed Rule," 79 *Federal Register*, pp. 1936 and 2063, January 10, 2014, http://www.gpo.gov/fdsys/pkg/FR-2014-01-10/pdf/2013-31497.pdf.

[97] The MIPPA required that, beginning with plan year 2010, the Secretary identify categories and classes of drugs for which both of the following criteria are met: 1) restricted access to drugs in the category or class would have major or life threatening clinical consequences for individuals who have a disease or disorder treated by the drugs in such category or class and 2) there is significant clinical need for such individuals to have access to multiple drugs within a category or class due to unique chemical actions and pharmacological effects of the drugs within the category or class. The ACA specified that the six drug categories or classes of clinical concern would remain in place until the Secretary established new criteria to

identify drug categories or classes of clinical concern under Section 1860D–4(b)(3)(G) of the Social Security Act through notice and rulemaking.

[98] CMS, MLN Matters, "Reimbursement for Vaccines and Vaccine Administration under Medicare Part D," Updated January 14, 2013, http://www.cms.gov/Outreach-and-Education/Medicare-Learning-Network-MLN/ MLNMattersArticles/downloads/se0727.pdf.

[99] Ibid, p. 5.

[100] CMS, "Vaccine Payments under Medicare Part D," June 2013, http://www.cms.gov /Outreach-and-Education/Medicare-Learning-Network-MLN/MLNProducts/Downloads/Vaccines-Part-D-Factsheet-ICN908764.pdf.

[101] CMS, *Medicare Prescription Drug Benefit Manual,* Chapter 6, "Part D Drugs and Formulary Requirements," Rev. February 19, 2010, http://www.cms.gov/Medicare/Prescription-Drug-Coverage/PrescriptionDrugCovContra/ Downloads/Chapter6.pdf.

[102] Plans may not remove covered Part D drugs from their formularies, or make any change in preferred or tiered cost- sharing status of a covered Part D drug, between the beginning of the annual coordinated election period October 15, and 60 days after the beginning of the contract year.

[103] 42 C.F.R. §423.153.

[104] Each plan negotiates the price of each drug with its manufacturer. If a plan obtains a good discount on one brand- name drug, but not on a competing drug used in treating the same condition, the plan may charge a lower co-pay for the former (preferred) drug and a higher co-pay for the latter (non-preferred).

[105] The co-insurance may be imposed until an enrollee reaches the Part D initial coverage limit. Sponsors that impose a zero or lower-than-standard plan deductible may impose a coinsurance of up to 33% for specialty tier drugs in order to maintain actuarial equivalence in basic benefits. Most plans charge the higher 33% rate. See Jack Hoadley, Laura Summer, Elizabeth Hargrave, Juliatte Cubanski, and Tricia Neuman, "*Medicare Part D in Its Ninth Year: The 2014 Marketplace and Key Trends, 2006-2014*," Kaiser Family Foundation, August 18, 2014, http://kff.org/medicare/report/ medicare-part-d-in-its-ninth-year-the-2014-marketplace-and-key-trends-2006-2014/.

[106] CMS, "2014 Final Call Letter," April 1, 2013, http://www.cms.gov/Medicare/Health-Plans/ MedicareAdvtgSpecRateStats/downloads/Announcement2014.pdf.

[107] Jack Hoadley, Laura Summer, Elizabeth Hargrave, Juliette Cubanski and Tricia Neuman, *Medicare Part D in Its Ninth Year: The 2014 Marketplace and Key Trends, 2006-2014*, Kaiser Family Foundation, August 18, 2014, http://kff.org/medicare/report/medicare-part-d-in-its-ninth-year-the-2014-marketplace-and-key-trends-2006-2014.

[108] CMS, *Medicare Prescription Drug Benefit Manual,* Chapter 6, "Part D Drugs and Formulary Requirements," Rev. February 19, 2010, Section 30.2, http://www.cms.gov /Medicare/Prescription-Drug-Coverage/ PrescriptionDrugCovContra/Downloads/Chapter6.pdf.

[109] The 2014 Humana/Walmart Rx Plan (PDP), https://www.humana.com/medicare/products-and-services/drug-plan/ 2014-prescription-drug-plan/walmart-preferred-rx.

[110] CMS, "2013 Prescription Drug Plans." Available in 2013 Landscape Presentations, at http://www.cms.gov/ Medicare/Prescription-Drug-Coverage/PrescriptionDrugCovGenIn /index.html?redirect=/PrescriptionDrugCovGenIn/.

[111] CMS, "Medicare Part D Specialty Tier," April 7, 2014, http://www.cms.gov/Medicare /Prescription-Drug-Coverage/PrescriptionDrugCovGenIn/Downloads/SpecialtyTier Methodology.pdf.

[112] 42 C.F.R. §423.153(b)(4)(i).

113 CMS, "Calendar Year 2013 Call Letter," Power Point Presentation, Slide 28, http://www.in.gov/idoi/files/SHIPPresentation_4.27.12.pdf.

114 CMS, "Changes to the Medicare Advantage and Medicare Prescription Drug Benefit Programs for Contract Year 2013 and Other Changes, Final Rule," 77 *Federal Register*, April 12, 2012, 22072-22175; http://www.gpo.gov/fdsys/ pkg/FR-2012-04-12/pdf/2012-8071.pdf.

115 Government Accountability Office, "Medicare Part D: Instances of Questionable Access to Prescription Drugs," September 2011, http://www.gao.gov/assets/590/585424.pdf.

116 CMS, "Medicare Part D Overutilization Monitoring System," July 5, 2013, http://www.cms.gov/Medicare/Prescription-Drug-Coverage/PrescriptionDrugCovContra /Downloads/HPMS-memo-Medicare-Part-D-Overutilization- Monitoring-System-07-05-13-.pdf.

117 Testimony of Gary Cantrell Deputy Inspector General for Investigations and Stuart Wright, Deputy Inspector General for Evaluation and Inspections, HHS Office of Inspector General, Senate Committee on Homeland Security and Governmental Affairs, June 24, 2013, https://oig.hhs.gov/testimony/docs/2013/ cantrell_wright_testimony_06242013.pdf.

118 CMS, Final Call Letter 2013, "Improving Drug Utilization Review Controls in Part D," http://www.cms.gov/Medicare/Prescription-Drug-Coverage/PrescriptionDrugCovContra /Downloads/Improving-DUR-Controls-in-Part- D.pdf. For a full list of CMS Guidance on this issue, see the CMS web page on Improving Drug Utilization Controls in Part D, http://www.cms.gov/Medicare/Prescription-Drug-Coverage/PrescriptionDrugCov Contra/RxUtilization.html.

119 CMS, "Medicare Part D Overutilization Monitoring System," July 5, 2013, http://www.cms.gov/Medicare/Prescription-Drug-Coverage/PrescriptionDrugCov Contra/Downloads/HPMS-memo-Medicare-Part-D-Overutilization- Monitoring-System-07-05-13-.pdf.

120 CMS, "Medicare Program; Contract Year 2015 Policy and Technical Changes to the Medicare Advantage and the Medicare Prescription Drug Benefit Programs; Final Rule," 79 *Federal Register*, May 23, 2014, pp. 29888-29906; http://www.gpo.gov/fdsys/pkg/FR-2014-05-23/pdf/2014-11734.pdf.

121 CMS Fact Sheet, "CY 2014 Medication Therapy Management Program Guidance and Submission Instructions," April 5, 2013. Available at http://www.cms.gov/Medicare /Prescription-Drug-Coverage/PrescriptionDrugCovContra/ MTM.html.

122 CMS, "CY 2014 Medication Therapy Management Program Guidance and Submission Instructions," April 5, 2013. Available at http://www.cms.gov/Medicare/Prescription-Drug-Coverage/PrescriptionDrugCovContra/MTM.html.

123 CMS, "2013 Medicare Part D Medication Therapy Management (MTM) Programs," p. 4, September 12, 2013, Available at http://www.cms.gov/Medicare/Prescription-Drug-Coverage/PrescriptionDrugCovContra/MTM.html. In January 2014, CMS proposed rules designed to increase MTM participation. CMS noted that that the share of beneficiaries enrolled in MTM programs has long lagged its 25% target. Under the proposed rules, Part D plans in 2015 would have to have a MTM outreach program, and would have to enroll beneficiaries who have two or more chronic conditions, with one being a core chronic disease; are taking two or more covered Part D drugs; and have drug costs in line with spending of beneficiaries who use two or more Part D-covered drugs. The annual drug spending threshold would initially be set at $620. See CMS, "Medicare Program; Contract Year 2015 Policy and Technical Changes to the Medicare Advantage and the Medicare Prescription Drug Benefit Programs; Proposed Rule," 79 *Federal Register*, p. 1953, January

10, 2014, http://www.gpo.gov/fdsys/pkg/FR-2014-01-10/pdf/2013-31497.pdfhttp://www.gpo.gov/fdsys/pkg/FR-2014-01-10/pdf/2013-31497.pdf. CMS did not finalize the rules but did include language in its final 2015 Call Letter spelling out steps it was taking to ensure plan sponsors were in compliance with MTM requirements. See CMS 2015 Final Call Letter, p. 119, http://www.cms.gov/ Medicare/Health-Plans/MedicareAdvtgSpecRateStats/Downloads/Announcement2015.pdf.

[124] The Part D sponsors are private entities licensed to offer health insurance under state law. Alternatively, they could meet solvency standards established by CMS for entities not licensed by the state.

[125] If two or more plans are not available in a region (one of which is a PDP), Medicare is required to contract with a non-risk "fallback" plan to serve beneficiaries in that area. Because of the large number of Part D plans participating in the program, CMS has not needed to solicit bids from fallback contractors.

[126] CMS, "Medicare 2013 Part D Landscape," Power Point Presentation, September 19, 2012. Access to presentation is at http://www.cms.gov/Medicare/Prescription-Drug-Coverage/PrescriptionDrugCovGenIn/index.html.

[127] CMS, "2014 Final Call Letter," April 1, 2013, http://www.cms.gov/Medicare/Health-Plans/MedicareAdvtgSpecRateStats/downloads/Announcement2014.pdf.

[128] Social Security Act, §1860D-11(i).

[129] CMS, "Medicare 2013 Part D Landscape," Power Point Presentation, September 19, 2012. Access to presentation is at http://www.cms.gov/Medicare/Prescription-Drug-Coverage/PrescriptionDrugCovGenIn/index.html.

[130] CMS, "Medicare 2013 Part D Landscape," Power Point Presentation, September 19, 2012. Access to presentation is at http://www.cms.gov/Medicare/Prescription-Drug-Coverage/PrescriptionDrugCovGenIn/index.html.

[131] Figures are based on Medicare Payment Advisory Commission, *2014 Report to Congress*, March 2014, p. 373, http://www.medpac.gov/documents/ Mar14_EntireReport.pdf.

[132] CMS, "2013 Medicare Part D Landscape," September 19, 2012. Access to presentation is at http://www.cms.gov/Medicare/Prescription-Drug-Coverage/PrescriptionDrugCovGenIn/index.html.

[133] The calculation of the national average monthly bid amount does not include bids submitted by Medical Savings Account (MSA) plans, MA private fee-for-service plans, specialized MA plans for special needs populations (SNP), Program of All-Inclusive Care for the Elderly (PACE) plans, or plans established through reasonable cost contracts.

[134] In 2006, the first year of Part D, there was no prior PDP enrollment information; therefore, each PDP plan was weighted equally (though MA-PD bids were enrollment-weighted if they had 2005 MA enrollment). Rather than immediately moving to full enrollment weighting in 2007, CMS provided for a phase-in under its demonstration authority. In 2007, 80% of the national monthly bid amount was based on the 2006 averaging methodology and 20% on the enrollment-weighted average. In 2008, 40% was based on the 2006 averaging methodology and 60% on the enrollment-weighted average. In 2009 and thereafter, the national bid amount is fully weighted by plan enrollment.

[135] CMS, "Annual Release of Part D National Average Bid Amount and other Part C & D Bid Related Information," July 30, 2013, http://www.cms.gov/Medicare/Health-Plans/MedicareAdvtgSpecRateStats/downloads/ PartDandMAbenchmarks2014.pdf.

[136] Social Security Act Section 1860D-15(e)(1)(B).

[137] The plan's standardized bid is their estimated cost of providing the standard Part D drug benefit. This bid is used in the calculation to determine plan payments.

[138] Social Security Act Section 1860D-15(e)(3)(B).

[139] Allowable costs include Part D drug costs minus the reinsurance subsidy and direct and indirect remuneration from drug manufacturers.

[140] CMS, "Advance Notice of Methodological Changes for Calendar Year (CY) 2015 for Medicare Advantage (MA) Capitation Rates, Part C and Part D Payment Policies and 2015 Call Letter," p. 34, February 21, 2014, http://www.cms.gov/Medicare/Health-Plans/MedicareAdvtgSpecRateStats/Downloads/Advance2015.pdf.

[141] CMS, 2014 Annual Report of the Boards of Trustees of the Federal Hospital Insurance and Federal Supplementary Medical Insurance Trust Funds, Table IV.B10, http://www.cms.gov/Research-Statistics-Data-and-Systems/Statistics-Trends-and-Reports /ReportsTrustFunds/downloads/tr2014.pdf.

[142] CMS, *2014 Initial Call Letter*, p. 34, http://www.cms.gov/Medicare/Health-Plans/MedicareAdvtgSpecRateStats/ Downloads/Advance2015.pdf.

[143] CMS, *Medicare Prescription Drug Manual*, Chapter 5, Section 50; http://www.cms.gov/Medicare/Prescription- Drug-Coverage/PrescriptionDrugCovContra /Downloads/MemoPDBManualChapter5_093011.pdf.

[144] CMS can waive the standards in the case of (1) MA-PD plans that operate their own pharmacies, provided they can demonstrate convenient access, and (2) private-fee-for-service plans offering Part D coverage for drugs purchased from all pharmacies, provided they do not charge additional cost sharing for drugs obtained from non-network pharmacies.

[145] CMS, *Medicare Prescription Drug Manual*, Chapter 5, Section 50.8.1; http://www.cms.gov/Medicare/Prescription-Drug-Coverage/PrescriptionDrugCovContra /Downloads/MemoPDBManualChapter5_093011.pdf.

[146] Because cost-sharing cannot be changed under defined standard coverage, such plans cannot have price differences based on the pharmacy used.

[147] The rules are waived in certain instances, such as MA-PD plans that offer access to drugs through retail pharmacies owned and operated by the MA organization that offers the plan. See CMS, *Medicare Prescription Drug Manual*, Chapter 5, Section 50.9, http://www.cms.gov/Medicare/Prescription-Drug-Coverage/PrescriptionDrugCovContra /Downloads/MemoPDBManualChapter5_093011.pdf.

[148] Ibid.

[149] CMS, "2013 Prescription Drug Plans," December 2012. See 2013 Landscape presentation at Prescription Drug Coverage, General Information, http://www.cms.gov/Medicare /Prescription-Drug- Coverage/PrescriptionDrugCovGenIn/index.html.

[150] CMS, "2014 Final Call Letter," p. 175, April 1, 2013, http://www.cms.gov/Medicare/Health-Plans/ MedicareAdvtgSpecRateStats/Downloads/Announcement2014.pdf.

[151] In January 2014, CMS published proposed rules that would have made major revisions in the pharmacy contracting process. In May 2014 CMS said it was not finalizing the rule. The proposed rules would have allowed a plan sponsor to offer preferred pricing through a subset of pharmacies only if 1) the preferred pricing were available to any willing pharmacy, and 2) the drugs have "consistently lower negotiated prices" than the same Part D drugs obtained in the rest of the plan's pharmacy network. See "Medicare Program; Contract Year 2015 Policy and Technical Changes to the Medicare Advantage and the Medicare Prescription Drug Benefit Programs; Proposed Rule," 79 *Federal Register*, p. 2063, January 10, 2014, http://www.gpo.gov/fdsys/pkg/FR-2014-01-10/pdf/2013-31497.pdf. CMS did not finalize the preferred pharmacy section of the proposed rules.

[152] CMS recognizes that the rural standard could be impracticable or impossible to meet in such areas, and will consider modifications in certain cases. CMS, *Medicare Prescription Drug*

Manual, Chapter 5, Section 50.10, http://www.cms.gov/Medicare/Prescription-Drug-Coverage/PrescriptionDrugCovContra/Downloads/MemoPDBManualChapter5_093011.pdf

[153] CMS, *Medicare Prescription Drug Manual*, Chapter 5, Sections 50.10 and 50.2, Rev. September 30, 2011, http://www.cms.gov/Medicare/Prescription-Drug-Coverage /PrescriptionDrugCovContra/Downloads/MemoPDBManualChapter5_093011.pdf.

[154] Ibid., Section 50.10. Sponsors may require an enrollee to pay higher cost-sharing up to an amount equal to the mail- order cost-sharing plus any differential in contracted rates between retail and mail-order, but plans may charge beneficiaries a lower cost sharing at retail if they so choose. Some pharmacies may ship drugs to patients in long-term care facilities or in rural areas. A pharmacy that makes some but not the predominance of its deliveries through the mail is not a mail-order pharmacy.

[155] MedPAC, *Report to the Congress: Medicare and the Health Care Delivery System*, Chapter 6, June 2012, http://www.medpac.gov/chapters/Jun12_Ch06.pdf.

[156] CMS, *Medicare Prescription Drug Manual*, Chapter 5, Section 60, Rev. September 30, 2011, http://www.cms.gov/Medicare/Prescription-Drug-Coverage/PrescriptionDrugCovContra /Downloads/MemoPDBManualChapter5_093011.pdf.

[157] This provision was added by MIPPA and may be found at Section 1860D-12(b)(4)(A)(ii) of the Social Security Act.

[158] CMS, *Medicare Appeals*, http://www.medicare.gov/Pubs/pdf/11525.pdf.

[159] CMS, *Medicare Part D Prescription Drug Manual*, Chapter 18, "Part D Enrollee Grievances, Coverage Determinations, and Appeals," Rev. February 22, 2013, http://cms.gov/Medicare/Appeals-and-Grievances/MedPrescriptDrugApplGriev/index.html.

[160] An enrollee may request a representative by using a government form (Form CMS-1696) or by submitting an equivalent written notice that includes information about enrollee and is signed and dated by both the enrollee and the representative. There are exceptions in the case of institutionalized or incapacitated enrollees.

[161] CMS, *Medicare Prescription Drug Manual*, Chapter 18, "Part D Enrollee Grievances, Coverage Determinations, and Appeals," Rev. February 22, 2013, Section 10.5, http://cms.gov/Medicare/Appeals-and-Grievances/ MedPrescriptDrugApplGriev/index.html.

[162] This includes a decision not to pay because the drug is not on the plan's formulary, the drug is determined not medically necessary, or the drug is furnished by an out-of-network pharmacy.

[163] MMA provided that if a Part D plan includes a tiered cost-sharing structure, a plan enrollee can request an exception to the structure. Under an exception, a non-preferred drug could be covered as a preferred drug if the prescribing physician determined that the preferred drug for treatment of the same condition would not be as effective for the individual, would have adverse effects for the individual, or both.

[164] MMA provided that a beneficiary enrolled in a Part D plan can appeal a determination not to provide coverage for a drug not on the plan's formulary. The appeal can only be made if the prescribing physician determines that all covered Part D drugs on any tier of the formulary for treatment of the same condition would not be as effective for the individual as the non-formulary drug, would have adverse effects for the individual, or both.

[165] CMS, *Medicare Prescription Drug Benefit Manual*, Chapter 18, "Part D Enrollee Grievances, Coverage Determinations, and Appeals," September 22, 2013, Section 40.2, available at http://cms.hhs.gov/Medicare/Appeals- and-Grievances/MedPrescriptDrugApplGriev/index. html.

[166] Ibid.

[167] Individuals can appeal coverage determinations related to formulary drugs and non-formulary drugs. They cannot appeal denial of coverage for excluded drugs.

[168] CMS, *Medicare Prescription Drug Benefit Manual*, Chapter 18, "Part D Enrollee Grievances, Coverage Determinations, and Appeals," September 22, 2013, Section 50.1, available at http://cms.hhs.gov/Medicare/Appeals-and-Grievances/MedPrescriptDrugApplGriev /index.html.

[169] If the issue is the denial of coverage based on medical necessity, the redetermination must be made by a physician.

[170] CMS, "Part D Fact Sheet," link to zip file available on Reconsideration page at http://www.cms.gov/Medicare/Appeals-and-Grievances/MedPrescriptDrugApplGriev/index.html.

[171] CMS, *Medicare Prescription Drug Benefit Manual*, Chapter 18, "Part D Enrollee Grievances, Coverage Determinations, and Appeals," September 22, 2013, Section 90.1, available at http://cms.hhs.gov/Medicare/Appeals- and-Grievances/MedPrescriptDrugAppl Griev/index. html.

[172] 42 C.F.R. §423.564.

[173] 42 C.F.R. §423.564.

[174] Social Security Act, §1154(a)(14).

[175] For more information, see CMS, "Quality Improvement Organizations," http://www.cms.gov/Medicare/Quality-Initiatives-Patient-Assessment-Instruments /QualityImprovementOrgs/index.html?redirect=/qualityimprovementorgs.

[176] The only statutorily required activity is that CMS conduct financial audits of one-third of the plans each year. Social Security Act Section 1860D-12(b)(3)(C).

[177] CMS, Program Audits, http://www.cms.gov/Medicare/Compliance-and-Audits/Part-C-and-Part-D-Compliance- and-Audits/Program-Audits.html; and CMS, *Prescription Drug Benefit Manual*, Chapter 9, Compliance Program Guidelines," p. 34, Rev. January 11, 2013, http://www.cms.gov/Regulations-and-Guidance/Guidance/Manuals/ Downloads/mc86c21.pdf.

[178] CMS, *Prescription Drug Benefit Manual*, Chapter 9, Compliance Program Guidelines," Rev. January 11, 2013, http://www.cms.gov/Regulations-and-Guidance/Guidance/Manuals /Downloads/mc86c21.pdf.

[179] Ibid.

[180] CMS, "Alert: New Fraud Awareness Tools for Part C and D Plan Sponsors," February 21, 2013, http://www.iceforhealth.org/library/documents/2013-0221_Alert_New_Fraud_ Awareness_Tools_for_Part_C_and_D_Plan_Sponsors.pdf.

[181] National Benefit Integrity Medicare Drug Integrity Contractor, http://www.healthintegrity.org /contracts/nbi-medic.

[182] CMS, *Prescription Drug Benefit Manual*, Chapter 9, "Compliance Program Guidelines," Section 50.7.4, Rev. January 11, 2013, http://www.cms.gov/Medicare/Prescription-Drug-Coverage/PrescriptionDrugCovContra/Downloads/ Chapter9.pdf.

[183] CMS, "Part D Recovery Audit Contractor," http://www.cms.gov/Research-Statistics-Data-and-Systems/Monitoring-Programs/recovery-audit-program-parts-c-and-d/Part-D-Recovery-Audit-Contractor.html.

[184] Government Accountability Office, *Medicare Part D Prescription Drug Coverage: Federal Oversight of Reported Price Concessions Data*, (GAO-08-1074R), September 30, 2008, http://www.gao.gov/products/GAO-08-1074R.

[185] Pharmacy benefit managers (PBM) are third-party administrators of prescription drug programs. The PBMs process prescriptions for insurers and other entities, create formularies, and negotiate drug prices with insurers and manufacturers.

[186] CMS, "Medicare Program; Changes to the Medicare Advantage and the Medicare Prescription Drug Benefit Programs for Contract Year 2013 and Other Changes; Final Rule," 77 *Federal Register*, p. 22171, April 12, 2012, http://www.gpo.gov/fdsys/pkg/FR-2012-04-12/pdf/2012-8071.pdf. Data to be reported include the total number of prescriptions dispensed, the share of prescriptions provided through retail rather than mail order pharmacies; the percentage of prescriptions for which a generic drug was available and dispensed, by pharmacy type; the aggregate amount and type of rebates, discounts, or price concessions (excluding bona fide service fees) that the PBM negotiates that are attributable to patient utilization under the plan; the aggregate amount of rebates, discounts, or price concessions that are passed through to the plan sponsor, and the total number of prescriptions dispensed; and the aggregate amount of the difference between the amount the Part D sponsor pays the PBM and the amount that the PBM pays retail pharmacies, and mail order pharmacies

[187] The MMA established within the Supplementary Medical Insurance (SMI) trust fund the Medicare Prescription Drug Account to be used in conjunction with the Part D prescription drug program. For additional information on Medicare program financing, see CRS Report R43122, *Medicare Financial Status: In Brief*, and CRS Report R41436, *Medicare Financing*, both by Patricia A. Davis.

[188] 2014 Annual Report of the Boards of Trustees of the Federal Hospital Insurance and Federal Supplementary Medical Insurance Trust Funds, July 28, 2014, Table III.D3, p. 109, http://www.cms.gov/Research-Statistics-Data-and-Systems/Statistics-Trends-and-Reports/ReportsTrustFunds/Downloads/TR2014.pdf.

[189] For example, the base premiums for 2014 were announced in July 2013. See CMS Memorandum, "Annual Release of Part D National Average Bid Amount and other Part C & D Bid Related Information," July 31, 2013, http://www.cms.gov/Medicare/Health-Plans/MedicareAdvtgSpecRateStats/Downloads/ PartDandMABenchmarks2014.pdf.

[190] The income thresholds are set at the same levels as those under Part B. For additional information, see Social Security Publication, *Medicare Premiums: Rules for Higher-Income Beneficiaries*, at http://www.ssa.gov/pubs/EN-05- 10536.pdf.

[191] Beginning in 2011, prescription drug manufacturers of brand name drugs provide a 50% discount for their drugs when used during the coverage gap. Medicare makes payments prospectively to non-employer Part D plan sponsors and is reimbursed for these amounts once the sponsors receive the discounts from the manufacturers. This discount reduces beneficiary out-of-pocket costs, but has little net effect on federal Part D spending.

[192] The October through December 2013 monthly per-capita amounts for each state may be found at http://www.medicaid.gov/Federal-Policy-Guidance/Downloads/Clawback-letter.pdf.

[193] 2014 Annual Report of the Boards of Trustees of the Federal Hospital Insurance and Federal Supplementary Medical Insurance Trust Funds, July 28, 2014; and Congressional Budget Office, Competition and the Cost of Medicare's Prescription Drug Program, July 2014, http://www.cbo.gov/sites/default/files/cbofiles/attachments/45552- PartD.pdf.

In: Medicare Part D Prescription Drug Benefit ISBN: 978-1-63482-524-5
Editor: Elena Marshall

Chapter 2

MEDICARE PROGRAM INTEGRITY: CMS PURSUES MANY PRACTICES TO ADDRESS PRESCRIPTION DRUG FRAUD, WASTE, AND ABUSE*

United States Government Accountability Office

ABBREVIATIONS

CMS	Centers for Medicare & Medicaid Services
CPARS	Contractor Performance Assessment Reports System
CPI	Center for Program Integrity
D&M	Detection and Monitoring
DEA	Drug Enforcement Administration
DUR	drug utilization review
FDR	First Tier, Downstream or Related Entity
HHS	Department of Health and Human Services
I&P	Investigation AND Prosecution
MEDIC	Medicare Drug Integrity Contractor
MMA	Medicare Prescription Drug, Improvement, and Modernization Act of 2003

* This is an edited, reformatted and augmented version of The United States Government Accountability Office publication, GAO-15-66, dated October 2014.

NBI	National Benefit Integrity
O&E	Outreach and Education
OIG	Office of Inspector General
OMS	Overutilization Monitoring System
PDMP	Prescription Drug Monitoring Program
RAC	Recovery Audit Contractor
SIU	Special Investigation Unit

WHY GAO DID THIS STUDY

Recent media reports and law enforcement actions have highlighted the problem of prescription drug fraud, waste, and abuse in the United States. Medicare, and the Part D prescription drug benefit, are susceptible to such fraud—a risk made greater by Medicare's size, scope, and complexity. GAO and others have raised questions about CMS's oversight of its activities to address fraud, waste, and abuse in Part D, as well as oversight of the contractors tasked with this work. GAO examined (1) practices for promoting prescription drug program integrity, and (2) the extent that CMS's oversight of Medicare Part D program integrity, including the program integrity contractors, reflects these practices. To develop a list of practices, GAO interviewed 14 stakeholder groups involved in various aspects of prescription drug program integrity, including provider, beneficiary, and anti-fraud groups; identified and reviewed related documents; and conducted a search of eight bibliographic databases that included peer-reviewed articles and government documents. GAO organized the practices based on the three categories of GAO's Fraud Prevention Framework. To determine how CMS's oversight reflects these practices, GAO analyzed agency documents, such as contracts, manuals, work products, and CMS audits of contractors; and interviewed agency officials.

WHAT GAO FOUND

GAO identified 23 practices for addressing prescription drug fraud, waste, and abuse that fall within three categories based on GAO's Fraud Prevention Framework—prevention, detection and monitoring, and investigation and prosecution.

Practices Implemented, Planned, and Not Pursued by CMS and Its Contractors to Address Prescription Drug Fraud, Waste, and Abuse

Category	Practice[a]	Implemented	Planned	Not pursuing
Prevention	Providing clinical guidelines			•
	Practicing collaboration	•		
	Educating clinicians and others	•		
	Using health information technology			•
	Limiting supply of abused drugs			•
	Using prepayment edits	•		
	Screening participants of health insurance programs	•		
	Using Prescription Drug Monitoring Programs (PDMP)[b]			•
Detection and monitoring	Providing clinical guidelines			•
	Practicing collaboration	•		
	Having compliance programs	•		
	Conducting data analysis	•		
	Conducting drug utilization reviews	•		
	Educating patients and others	•		
	Limiting certain patients to certain providers ("lock-ins")			•
	Using PDMPs[b]		•	
	Conducting postpayment reviews	•		
Investigation and prosecution	Practicing collaboration	•		
	Educating law enforcement and others	•		
	Pursuing enforcement options		•	
	Having investigative staff	•		
	Reporting to law enforcement	•		
	Using PDMPs[b]		•	

Source: GAO analysis of relevant literature, CMS documents, and interviews with CMS officials. | GAO-15-66.

[a] GAO determined that CMS had implemented a practice if the agency required or documented at least one activity within that practice, that CMS planned a practice if documentation or officials described activities as pilots or in the process of development, and that CMS was not pursuing a practice based on reviews of documentation and interviews with officials.

[b] PDMPs are state-based programs that operate electronic databases that gather information from pharmacies on certain dispensed prescriptions, such as whether a patient has multiple opioid prescriptions from multiple providers.

The Department of Health and Human Services' (HHS) Centers for Medicare & Medicaid Services' (CMS) activities to address prescription drug fraud, waste, and abuse in the Medicare Part D prescription drug program reflect 14 of these 23 identified practices, some of which are in multiple categories, and the agency plans to implement 3 additional practices.

HHS generally agreed with our findings.

* * *

October 24, 2014

The Honorable Kevin Brady
Chairman
Subcommittee on Health
Committee on Ways and Means House of Representatives

Dear Mr. Chairman:

Recent media reports and law enforcement actions have highlighted the problem of prescription drug fraud, waste, and abuse in the United States.[1] Examples of problematic activities include beneficiaries "doctor shopping" to receive multiple prescriptions for opioids, such as OxyContin or Vicodin, from different providers; providers found to have questionable prescribing and billing practices; and diversion of prescription drugs by beneficiaries, pharmacies, and others for uses other than intended. Medicare and its prescription drug benefit, Part D, are susceptible to such fraud—a risk made greater by Medicare's size, scope, and complexity.[2]

Since 2006, the Part D program has provided voluntary, outpatient prescription drug coverage to the Medicare population. In 2013, Part D had nearly 40 million beneficiaries and cost almost $70 billion, or about 12 percent of total Medicare expenditures. The program is administered by the Centers for Medicare & Medicaid Services (CMS), within the Department of Health and Human Services (HHS). CMS contracts with private companies to provide benefits under Part D.

GAO, the HHS Office of Inspector General (OIG), and others have raised questions about CMS's oversight of its activities to address fraud, waste, and abuse in Part D, as well as oversight of the contractors tasked with assisting in these activities, the Medicare Drug Integrity Contractors (MEDIC).[3] You asked us to examine practices for addressing fraud, waste, and abuse in prescription drug programs, and CMS's use of these practices. We examined (1) practices for promoting prescription drug program integrity, and (2) the extent that CMS's oversight of Medicare Part D program integrity, including the MEDICs, reflects these practices.

To develop a list of practices for addressing prescription drug fraud, waste, and abuse, we interviewed stakeholders involved in prescription drug program integrity, such as groups representing prescribers, pharmacies, beneficiaries, and others, to discuss program integrity practices and identify documents that describe such practices. [4] Through these interviews we identified an initial 213 documents that appeared to address program integrity practices related to prescription drug fraud, waste, and abuse. We reviewed each document to identify specific practices and any relevant activities within those practices. We then conducted an additional search of eight bibliographic databases that included peer-reviewed articles and government documents that yielded an additional 642 documents that appeared to address program integrity practices related to prescription drug fraud, waste, and abuse. We reviewed the most recently published 10 percent, or 64 documents, to determine whether they were relevant and if they described additional specific practices not already determined through our review of the initial 213 documents. We did not identify any significantly different practices and therefore discontinued our review of documents. We reviewed, in total, 277 documents. We used GAO's Fraud Prevention Framework to organize the prescription drug program integrity practices we identified in our review into one of three categories: prevention, detection and monitoring, and investigation and prosecution.[5] We did not evaluate the practices we identified for their relative effectiveness.

To determine the extent to which CMS's oversight of Medicare Part D, including the MEDICs, reflects the practices we identified, we interviewed agency officials involved in the oversight of the MEDICs and plan sponsors. We also analyzed agency documents, such as the MEDIC contracts and manuals; MEDIC work products, including the MEDICs' most recent performance evaluations; plan sponsor contract materials and memos; CMS findings from its 2013 audits of selected plan sponsors; and CMS regulations. We used the reviewed materials and interviews with CMS officials to determine which of the practices we identified that CMS incorporates into its oversight of the Part D program, as well as the practices CMS does not incorporate or plans to incorporate in the future. We determined that CMS had implemented a practice if the agency required or documented at least one activity within that practice, that CMS planned a practice if documentation or officials described activities as pilots or in the process of development, and that CMS was not pursuing practices based on reviews of documentation and interviews with officials.

We conducted this performance audit from January 2014 to October 2014 in accordance with generally accepted government auditing standards.

Those standards require that we plan and perform the audit to obtain sufficient, appropriate evidence to provide a reasonable basis for our findings and conclusions based on our audit objectives. We believe that the evidence obtained provides a reasonable basis for our findings and conclusions based on our audit objectives.

BACKGROUND

Part D Plan Sponsors

The Medicare Part D program was designed to be administered by private organizations—referred to as plan sponsors—that CMS contracts with to provide outpatient prescription drug benefit plans to Medicare beneficiaries.[6] These sponsors may contract with other entities—called First Tier, Downstream or Related Entities (FDR)—to help provide these benefits. (See fig. 1.) FDRs include pharmacy benefit managers— companies that provide services such as contracting with a network of pharmacies, managing formularies, and performing drug utilization reviews on behalf of the sponsors—and pharmacies. CMS holds plan sponsors responsible for oversight of their FDRs.

Part D Program Integrity

Program integrity responsibilities in Medicare Part D are shared by plan sponsors, CMS's Center for Program Integrity (CPI) and Center for Medicare, and CMS's program integrity contractors.

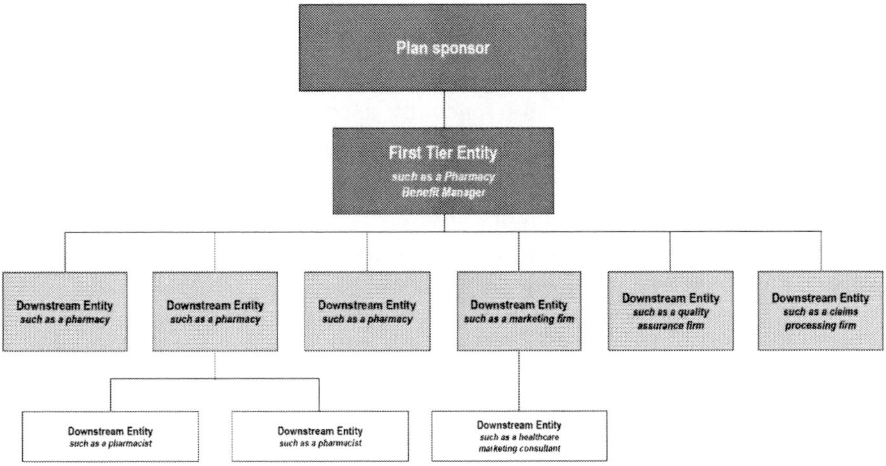

Source: GAO analysis of CMS information.| GAO-15-66.

Figure 1. Example of How a Part D Plan Sponsor Contracts with Other Entities.

Plan Sponsors' Responsibilities

Plan sponsors are required to have comprehensive compliance programs that include elements intended to safeguard the Part D program from fraud, waste, and abuse.[7] CMS issued requirements for these programs based on input from various sources, including plan sponsors and industry representatives.[8] CMS requires plan sponsors to

- monitor and audit their FDRs;
- analyze data to detect and prevent potential fraud, waste, and abuse; and
- have a unit, such as a Special Investigation Unit (SIU), specifically tasked with identifying and addressing fraud, waste, and abuse, or ensure that the responsibilities generally conducted by an SIU are conducted by a plan sponsor's compliance department.

CMS's Oversight

CMS's CPI oversees Part D program integrity and coordinates with other groups within CMS's Center for Medicare that monitor plan sponsor compliance with the Part D program. (See fig. 2.) Within the Center for Medicare, one such group is the Medicare Parts C and D Oversight and Enforcement Group, which ensures contractual compliance through audits of plan sponsors. If those audits identify noncompliance with the terms of the Part D contract, CMS may take a variety of actions that include requiring corrective action plans, sending warning letters, assessing civil money penalties, and terminating or not renewing a contract. The other group, the Medicare Drug Benefit and C & D Data Group, analyzes data to identify potential patient safety concerns, such as overutilization of opioid drugs, that may also indicate potential fraud or abuse.

CPI has primary responsibility for overseeing the two MEDICs tasked with promoting program integrity in Medicare Part D:[9]

- The National Benefit Integrity (NBI) MEDIC is responsible for preventing, detecting, and deterring Part D fraud, waste, and abuse. This includes intake and handling of complaints from beneficiaries and others as well as requests for information from law enforcement; investigating providers and others and referring them to law enforcement; and analyzing Part D program prescription drug event records and other data to identify patterns indicative of potential fraud, waste, or abuse.[10]
- The Outreach & Education (O&E) MEDIC provides Part D fraud, waste, and abuse education to plan sponsors and other stakeholders by working in concert with CMS to develop educational and training tools, and by facilitating information-sharing opportunities, such as fraud alerts, conferences, and other meetings.

CPI also oversees the Part D Recovery Audit Contractor (RAC) program, which is tasked with reviewing paid Medicare claims—or, for Part D, prescription drug event data—from plan sponsors and their pharmacies to determine overpayments and underpayments; providing information to CPI to help prevent future improper payments; and referring any potential fraud identified during the auditing process to the NBI MEDIC to investigate. While the Part D RAC may conduct work similar to the NBI MEDIC, the focus of the RAC is improper payments—such as overpayments—while the MEDIC's focus is potential fraud, waste, and abuse.

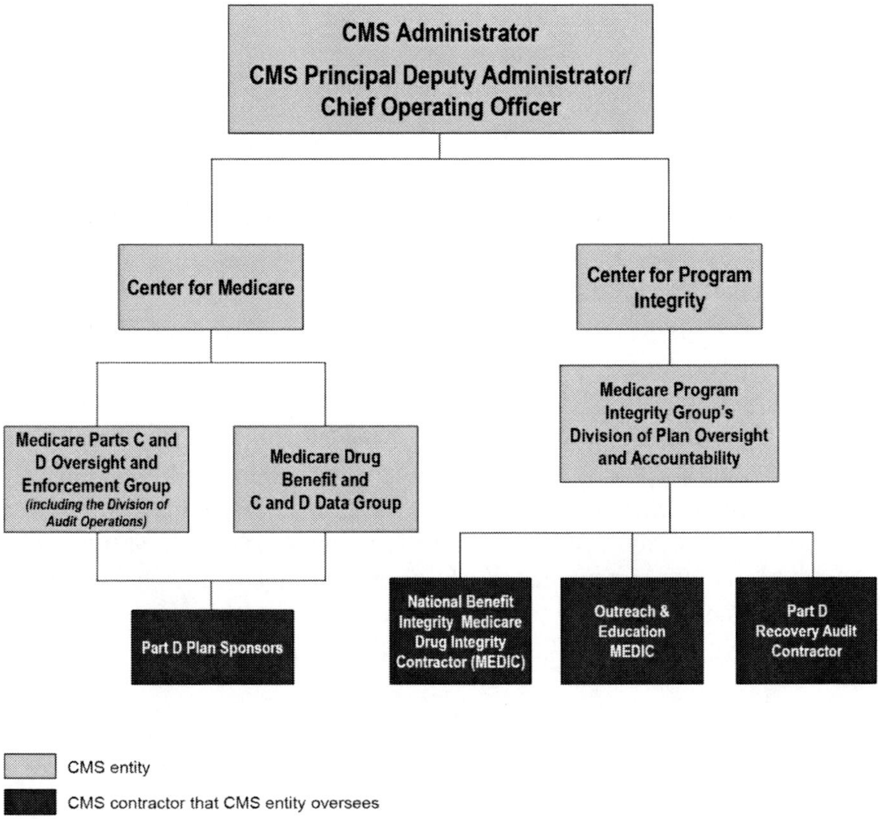

Source: GAO analysis of CMS information.| GAO-15-66.

Figure 2. CMS Entities with Primary Responsibility for Part D Plan Sponsor Oversight.

We Identified Multiple Prevention, Detection, and Investigation Practices to Address Prescription Drug Fraud, Waste, and Abuse

We identified a total of 23 practices for addressing prescription drug fraud, waste, and abuse that fall within one or more of the three categories based on the Fraud Prevention Framework: (1) prevention, (2) detection and monitoring, and (3) investigation and prosecution. Counting only once the practices that fall within more than one category, we identified 16 unique practices.

Prevention

We identified eight practices related to the prevention of prescription drug fraud, waste, and abuse that can include multiple activities, as shown in table 1. For example, one prevention practice, limiting the supply of abused drugs, can help prevent abuse by restricting the amount of potentially abused drugs that are available. This is done by conducting the following activities:

- offering "take-back" programs where patients can safely dispose of any unused medications, preventing use or abuse by others;
- securing information and materials, such as Drug Enforcement Administration (DEA) registration numbers and prescription pads,[11] that could prevent bad actors from illegally obtaining prescription drugs; and
- developing abuse-resistant drugs that could hamper efforts to abuse them.

Table 1. Prevention Practices for Prescription Drug Fraud, Waste, and Abuse

Practice	Description/examples
Clinical guidelines	Providing clinical guidance to prescribers and pharmacies regarding topics such as • using the lowest effective dose and judicious prescribing; • encouraging use of generic drugs as alternatives to brand drugs; • alternatives to opioid drugs, such as physical therapy; and • appropriate prescribing of noncontrolled substances, such as to reduce inappropriate prescribing of antibiotics.
Collaboration	Establishing mutually reinforcing or joint strategies among stakeholders when developing programs and/or strategies to address prevention of prescription drug fraud, waste, and abuse.
Education	Providing education or training to clinicians, patients, and others on how to prevent abuse, such as • training clinicians on appropriate prescribing of opioid drugs and • educating the public on correct use and safe disposal of prescription drugs.

Practice	Description/examples
Health information technology	Adopting health information technology, such as • electronic prescribing and • electronic health records.
Limit the supply of abused drugs	Limiting the supply of abused drugs, including • "take back" programs for safe prescription drug disposal; • physical and information security, including o safe storage of drugs; o safeguarding Drug Enforcement Administration, Medicare National Provider Identifier, andother identifiers that can be used to obtain prescription drugs fraudulently; o securing the prescription drug supply chain; and o restricting distribution of certain prescription drugs to appropriate entities; • developing abuse-resistant drugs, including generic versions; and • prescription verification (by provider or pharmacist), including o using tamper-resistant prescription pads, o checking patients' identification prior to dispensing certain drugs, and o verifying certain prescriptions with the prescriber.
Prepayment edits	Using prepayment edits—controls built into payment systems—to deny claims that should not be paid or to flag claims for additional review before payment.
Prescription Drug Monitoring Programs (PDMP)[a]	Having clinicians use their states' PDMPs to ensure patients are not inappropriately receiving multiple prescriptions, including • prescribers checking PDMPs prior to first prescribing certain prescription drugs and • pharmacists checking PDMPs prior to dispensing those drugs.
Screening	Screening the eligibility of beneficiaries, prescribers, pharmacies, and other entities to ensure that they have coverage under or participate in a health insurance program. (Note: This does not include screening for potential drug abuse.)

Source: GAO analysis of relevant literature. | GAO-15-66.

[a] PDMPs are state-based programs that operate electronic databases that gather information from pharmacies on certain dispensed prescriptions. Authorized users access the information about a patient's prescription drug history, such as whether a patient has multiple opioid prescriptions from multiple providers.

Detection and Monitoring

We identified nine practices related to the detection and monitoring of prescription drug fraud, waste, and abuse, as shown in table 2. For example, the collaboration practice includes sharing information about specific fraud schemes and potentially fraudulent providers that can help other interested parties—such as other insurers—find those schemes and providers within their own systems. These practices also help monitor individuals who have been identified as potentially abusing drugs or health care benefits. For example, one practice we identified is recipient restriction programs—called "lock-ins"—that typically require certain patients to use one prescribing physician and one dispensing pharmacy— to better track their prescription drug use.

Table 2. Detection and Monitoring Practices for Prescription Drug Fraud, Waste, and Abuse

Practice	Description/examples
Clinical guidelines	Providing clinical guidance to prescribers and pharmacies regarding topics such as • screening patients for potential drug abuse, such as through urine testing or other screening tools, and • more frequent evaluations of patients who are prescribed certain drugs.
Collaboration	Establishing mutually reinforcing or joint strategies among stakeholders to help in detection and monitoring efforts, such as sharing information on specific fraud schemes, results of data analysis, and disciplinary actions taken against providers.
Compliance program	Establishing effective compliance programs that include the following elements: • written policies, procedures, and standards of conduct; • designation of a compliance officer and committee; • effective training and education; • effective lines of communication; • enforcing standards; • internal monitoring and auditing; and • responding promptly to offenses and developing corrective actions.
Data analysis	Having dedicated and appropriate staff for collecting and actively analyzing data to identify outliers or other markers of potential fraud, waste, or abuse.
Drug utilization review (DUR)	Having authorized, structured, ongoing reviews of prescribing, dispensing, and use of medication, which can include • prospective reviews, such as requiring prior authorization for certain drugs, high drug doses, or large drug quantities before the drugs are dispensed; • concurrent reviews; and

Practice	Description/examples
	• retrospective or retroactive reviews.
Education	Educating insurers, providers, patients, and others on how to detect potential prescription drug fraud, waste, and abuse. This can include alerting providers to their prescribing patterns.
Postpayment reviews	Reviewing claims and other documents after payment to ensure compliance with payment rules and that the prescription was medically necessary, including the ability to suspend payments and obtain and review medical records. Alerting providers and beneficiaries to potential errors in services provided or received, such as by sending explanation of benefit reports to beneficiaries for their review.
Prescription Drug Monitoring Programs (PDMP)[a]	Using PDMP reports to help detect potential problems, which can be solicited reports, such as prescribers requesting a report about a particular patient, or unsolicited reports, such as a PDMP system automatically sending a prescriber a report on his or her patients and prescribing patterns.
Recipient restriction programs ("lock- ins")	Requiring certain patients—such as those at risk for abusing drugs, high-users of controlled substances, and others—typically to use only one prescribing physician and one dispensing pharmacy.

Source: GAO analysis of relevant literature. | GAO-15-66.

[a] PDMPs are state-based programs that operate electronic databases that gather information from pharmacies on certain dispensed prescriptions. Authorized users access the information about a patient's prescription drug history, such as whether a patient has multiple opioid prescriptions from multiple providers.

Investigation and Prosecution

We identified six practices related to the investigation and prosecution of prescription drug fraud, waste, and abuse, as shown in table 3. Practices include having investigative staff knowledgeable of prescription drug schemes and experienced in investigating them, as well as having the ability to take actions to enforce prescription drug rules.

CMS's Part D Program Integrity Efforts Reflect Many of the Practices We Identified

CMS pursues many of the practices we identified that can be used to prevent, detect, and investigate prescription drug fraud, waste, and abuse. In addition, CMS plans to add new and strengthen certain existing practices, but will not adopt certain other practices for a variety of reasons.

Table 3. Investigation and Prosecution Practices for Prescription Drug Fraud, Waste, and Abuse

Practice	Description/examples
Collaboration	Participating in joint investigations, task forces, and other investigative efforts. Sharing information, as appropriate, regarding ongoing fraud investigations, including information about the providers under investigation.
Education	Providing education to law enforcement and other investigators on how to investigate prescription drug fraud, waste, and abuse.
Enforcement	Having and using punitive measures against those involved in potential fraud, waste, or abuse of prescription drugs, such as • restricting providers' or beneficiaries' access to or removing them from insurance programs and • pursuing prosecutions.
Investigations/investigative staff	Having in-house investigators, such as a Special Investigative Unit, which take investigative steps such as on-site audits, medical record reviews, and other actions.
Prescription Drug Monitoring Programs (PDMP)[a]	Accessing and/or analyzing PDMP data in support of investigations and/or prosecutions.
Reporting to law enforcement	Reporting suspect bad actors and problems to law enforcement agencies.

Source: GAO analysis of relevant literature. | GAO-15-66.

[a] PDMPs are state-based programs that operate electronic databases that gather information from pharmacies on certain dispensed prescriptions. Authorized users access the information about a patient's prescription drug history, such as whether a patient has multiple opioid prescriptions from multiple providers.

CMS, with Its Contractors, Has Implemented Many Program Integrity Practices, Particularly within the Categories of Detection and Monitoring and Investigation and Prosecution

CMS activities to address prescription drug fraud, waste, and abuse reflect 14 of the 23 total practices we identified, based on interviews with officials and review of agency documents. Most of the practices CMS pursues—10 of its 14 practices—relate to the detection and monitoring, and investigation and prosecution categories.

CMS implements its prescription drug program integrity practices by assigning activities to and working with plan sponsors, the MEDICs, and others. For example,

- for prevention, CMS works with the O&E MEDIC to develop educational materials that plan sponsors can download from the O&E MEDIC's website and customize for their beneficiaries;
- for detection and monitoring, CMS requires plan sponsors to have compliance programs, which incorporate multiple practices we identified, such as data analysis, collaboration, and education; the NBI MEDIC also analyzes data and shares the results with plan sponsors; and
- for investigations and prosecutions, plan sponsors and the NBI MEDIC are expected to have staff who can identify and investigate potential fraud, waste, and abuse.

The NBI and O&E MEDICs reported completing work for a variety of practices, and CMS rated elements of the MEDICs' work from satisfactory to exceptional on their most recent performance assessments.[12]

NBI MEDIC

CMS paid approximately $17 million in 2013 to the NBI MEDIC to analyze data, process and review complaints, and develop investigations to promote Part D program integrity. In the most recently completed contract year, the NBI MEDIC reported the following:

- processing almost 7,000 complaints to determine whether they identified potential fraud, for which CMS most recently rated the contractor "exceptional";
- completing 7 data analysis projects and initiating 41 new projects, for which CMS most recently rated the contractor "exceptional"; and
- referring almost 400 cases that represented approximately $5.1 billion in potential fraud to law enforcement, for which CMS most recently rated the contractor "satisfactory" for its investigations and "exceptional" for its law enforcement referrals.[13]

O&E MEDIC

CMS paid approximately $1.7 million in 2013 to the O&E MEDIC to provide outreach and education that assists CMS in communicating program integrity efforts as well as supporting fraud, waste, and abuse oversight audits. In the most recently completed contract year, the O&E MEDIC reported the following:

- developing 59 outreach and education materials, such as fraud awareness flyers and frequently asked questions;
- developing 33 training products, such as webinars and job aids; and
- executing 8 conferences, including with stakeholders we interviewed, and providing 22 presentations at other conferences and meetings.
- CMS rated each element of the O&E MEDIC's work as "satisfactory."[14]

Table 4 identifies the practices implemented by CMS and its contractors.

Table 4. Practices Implemented by CMS and Its Contractors for Addressing Prescription Drug Fraud, Waste, and Abuse Category

Category	Practice	Responsible entities and examples of activities[a]
Prevention	Collaboration (prevention)	CMS has established relationships with a variety of stakeholders to help develop programs and strategies to address prescription drug fraud, waste, and abuse, including, for example, the agency's participation in the Public-Private Partnership to Prevent Health Care Fraud and as a member of the National Health Care Anti-Fraud Association.
	Education (prevention)	Outreach & Education Medicare Drug Integrity Contractor (O&E MEDIC), in concert with CMS Center for Program Integrity, offers a variety of materials and events, such as an insert on safe drug disposal that plan sponsors can provide to their beneficiaries, and training to Medicare beneficiaries on how to prevent potential fraud.
	Prepayment edits	Plan sponsors may implement edits at the point of sale to control specific beneficiaries' access to certain medications (see also drug utilization review (DUR) below). For every prescription, plan sponsors must check a range of information, typically at the point of sale or distribution, such as drug interactions, incorrect amounts, and age or gender contraindications, such as a woman

Category	Practice	Responsible entities and examples of activities[a]
		receiving medications prescribed only to men.
	Screening	Plan sponsors must verify beneficiaries' Part D eligibility. CMS finalized a rule in May 2014 establishing a Medicare enrollment requirement for Part D prescribers effective June 1, 2015, and strengthening screening for ineligible incarcerated beneficiaries starting January 1, 2015.[b]
Detection and monitoring (D&M)	Collaboration (D&M)	Plan sponsors are to share information with CMS regarding potentially fraudulent providers or schemes. National Benefit Integrity (NBI) and O&E MEDICs convene conferences and share information on prescription drug fraud, waste, and abuse with plan sponsors, law enforcement, beneficiaries, and other stakeholders. CMS sends memos to all plan sponsors about new Part D fraud schemes and potentially fraudulent providers that are also made available on the O&E MEDIC website. In addition, CMS sends the results of the NBI MEDIC's data analyses directly toa plan sponsor if the NBI MEDIC identifies particular issues for that sponsor to address.
	Compliance program	Plan sponsors are to have effective compliance programs.
	Data analysis	The NBI MEDIC conducts data analysis projects, such as identifying deceased prescribers across all plan sponsors, and is to have clinical and analytic staff to conduct that work. The NBI MEDIC is also implementing predictive analytic models to identify potential fraud in the Part D program. Plan sponsors are to have clinical and analytic staff, or contract with an entity that can provide such staff, to monitor and analyze data as part of their compliance programs.
	Drug utilization review (DUR)	Plan sponsors are to review beneficiaries' drug utilization patterns to identify potential patient harm and beneficiaries at risk for overutilization, and refer those beneficiaries for case management. Plan sponsors are to share information on these beneficiaries when they move from one Part D plan to another. CMS also reports quarterly to plan sponsors the names of beneficiaries overutilizing opioids and certain other drugs through CMS's Overutilization Monitoring System. Plan sponsors must report to CMS quarterly on how each identified case is addressed.

Table 4. (Continued)

Category	Practice	Responsible entities and examples of activities[a]
	Education (D&M)	O&E MEDIC, in coordination with CMS and the NBI MEDIC, provides training and materials to plan sponsors and others on how to identify potential fraud, waste, and abuse. For example, the O&E MEDIC, with CMS oversight, developed a Fraud Handbook that plan sponsors can access to learn about practical techniques and approaches on preventing, detecting, and investigating potential prescription drug fraud.
	Postpayment reviews	Plan sponsors are to conduct certain postpayment reviews (see also DUR above). Plan sponsors are also to provide beneficiaries with an explanation-of-benefits document to review for potential errors that also has a telephone number to report potential fraud. Part D Recovery Audit Contractor is to review paid Part D claims to identify over- and underpayments and recoup overpayments, and refer potential fraud identified during that postpayment review to the NBI MEDIC.
Investigation and prosecution (I&P)	Collaboration (I&P)	The NBI MEDIC responds to law enforcement requests for information and has participated in task forces and other investigative efforts. The O&E MEDIC trains insurance investigators, law enforcement, and others. CMS hosts quarterly meetings with a variety of stakeholders on prescription drug fraud, waste, and abuse.
	Education (I&P)	O&E MEDIC, in consultation with the NBI MEDIC, provides educational materials on how to investigate potential fraud.
	Investigations/ investigative staff	Plan sponsors are to have staff who can identify potential fraud. The NBI MEDIC is to have investigative staff knowledgeable of prescription drug fraud.
	Reporting to law enforcement	The NBI MEDIC is required to refer investigations to law enforcement. CMS encourages but does not require plan sponsors to refer potential fraud to law enforcement and/or CMS, including the NBI MEDIC.[c]

Source: GAO analysis of CMS documents and interviews with CMS officials. | GAO-15-66.

[a] This table does not include all instances of CMS's activities to implement the practices we identified.

[b] Once prescribers are enrolled, the rule provides that CMS will be able to revoke prescriber billing privileges for certain abuses of the program or noncompliance with applicable licensure requirements. To implement the exclusion of incarcerated individuals from Part D coverage, the rule redefined eligible Medicare service areas to exclude facilities in which individuals are incarcerated. See Medicare Program: Contract Year 2015 Policy and Technical Changes to the Medicare Advantage and the Medicare Prescription Drug Benefit Programs. 79 Fed. Reg. 29,844 (May 23, 2014).

[c] In a March 2014 report, OIG reiterated previous recommendations that it had made to CMS to amend regulations to require Part D plan sponsors to report to CMS their identification of and response to potential fraud and abuse incidents. CMS did not concur with this recommendation, citing concerns about creating duplicative reporting. See Department of Health and Human Services Office of Inspector General, Less than Half of Part D Sponsors Voluntarily Reported Data on Potential Fraud and Abuse, OEI-03-13-00030 (Washington, D.C.: March 2014). CMS officials told us in September 2014 that if the agency were to impose such a requirement, it would be able to evaluate sponsors' compliance with the reporting requirement, but not whether the reports identified actual fraud as defined by law enforcement.

CMS May Adopt Some Practices, but Not Others, for a Number of Reasons

CMS is planning to implement another 3 of the 23 total practices and to strengthen 4 that it has already implemented, but officials stated that the agency is not pursuing 6 practices for a number of reasons.

The three additional practices CMS plans to implement are the following:

- *Detection and Monitoring: Prescription Drug Monitoring Program (PDMP)*. CMS officials said the agency is seeking access to PDMP data through several avenues.[15] For example, CMS and the NBI MEDIC are working with the PDMP Center of Excellence to obtain de-identified PDMP data to assist the MEDIC in detecting potential patterns of prescription drug fraud, waste, and abuse.
- *Investigation and Prosecution: PDMPs*. CMS officials said CMS and the NBI MEDIC are also working with four states—Idaho, Indiana, Massachusetts, and New York—to obtain PDMP data as another data source to help investigate potential prescription drug diversion. Idaho currently is the only state that allows Medicare access to its PDMP,

while the other states have expressed interest in providing information to CMS.

- *Investigation and Prosecution: Enforcement.* Under the recently issued rule, which established a Medicare enrollment requirement for prescribers of drugs covered by Part D,[16] CMS can revoke a physician's or eligible professional's Medicare enrollment if the DEA or a state agency has suspended or revoked the individual's prescriber privileges. CMS may also revoke enrollment where it determines the individual has prescribing patterns or conducts practices that are abusive or represent a threat to the health and safety of Medicare beneficiaries, or both. Prior to this new requirement, CMS could not directly take administrative actions against a Part D provider. CMS officials also reported that they are working with OIG on how best to pursue other enforcement options, such as "permissive exclusions," which allow OIG to exclude providers from federal health programs for certain other actions, such as misdemeanor convictions for certain offenses.[17]

CMS is planning to strengthen four practices that it has already implemented, which correspond to all three categories.

- *Prevention: Screening.* CMS issued a final rule in May 2014 that is intended to strengthen Part D prescriber and beneficiary screening. The rule establishes a Medicare enrollment requirement for prescribers of drugs covered by Part D, effective June 2015.[18] As a result, CMS is to screen these prescribers during the Medicare enrollment process to verify that they meet specific requirements, such as having current licenses or accreditation and valid Social Security numbers. Additionally, this final rule authorizes CMS to revoke a physician's or eligible professional's Medicare enrollment for certain abuses of the program, or based upon a suspension or revocation of the prescriber's DEA certificate or state authority to prescribe drugs. As with fee-for-service providers, CMS will revalidate enrollment information when changes or updates are submitted and during a 5-year revalidation process. CMS is still considering whether to require pharmacies that dispense covered Part D drugs to enroll into the Medicare program.

  The rule is also intended to strengthen screening of Part D beneficiaries. 19 Currently, plan sponsors are to verify beneficiaries'

Part D eligibility. While incarcerated or confined beneficiaries are generally ineligible for Part D coverage, recent OIG reports found that CMS paid for prescription drugs for such beneficiaries.[20] The new rule implements the exclusion of beneficiaries incarcerated for 30 days or more from receiving Part D benefits starting January 1, 2015, by removing the facilities where individuals are incarcerated from the definition of a plan's service area.

- *Detection and Monitoring: Collaboration.* CMS is seeking to strengthen collaboration through a new voluntary web-based system created by the NBI MEDIC—PLATO—that is intended to allow CMS and plan sponsors to more easily share information on fraud schemes and potential bad actors. 21 For example, plan sponsors may use the system to share information on specific suspect providers so that other plan sponsors can determine whether they should also investigate or take actions against those providers. CMS officials said that they anticipate that PLATO will be accessible to plan sponsors by the end of 2014. In addition, according to agency officials, CMS is working with the NBI MEDIC to develop and implement predictive models in PLATO to help identify potential fraud schemes that can be shared with plan sponsors, such as a model for identifying prescribers who provide certain controlled substances to patients without a valid medical need.
- *Detection and Monitoring: Compliance Program.* CMS is pursuing options for improving its oversight of plan sponsors' compliance programs. In 2013, among the plan sponsors that it audited, CMS found weaknesses in the majority of plan sponsors' compliance programs for addressing fraud, waste, and abuse. During that year, CMS audited 29 plan sponsors, representing 14 percent of all plan sponsors and, of those, nearly all (94 percent) had findings related to fraud, waste, and abuse activities, according to officials.[22] These officials also reported that almost all weaknesses were addressed through a corrective action plan.[23] In January 2014, CMS proposed a rule that would require, among other things, that plan sponsors hire an independent auditor to verify that any required corrective action plans addressed deficiencies found during a program audit.[24] CMS did not finalize this requirement in the final rule issued in May 2014, and as of October 2014, CMS officials did not provide a proposed completion date.

In addition, CMS officials reported that the agency has an initiative under way to gather information that could help improve oversight of plan sponsors' practices to address fraud, waste, and abuse. As part of this initiative, CMS interviewed five plan sponsors about how they use the information CMS provided to them on new fraud schemes and potentially fraudulent providers. Based on this information, CMS officials reported that they could change how the agency audits plan sponsors' fraud, waste, and abuse activities, or increase the requirements for sponsors' activities, in order to improve oversight.[25] However, CMS officials noted that any changes will be based on the agency's final assessment of lessons learned from the initiative, which was still in progress as of August 2014.

- *Investigation and Prosecution: Collaboration.* CMS is working to develop a more formal way to share information about fraudulent providers with relevant state medical boards, CMS officials said, so that the medical boards can conduct additional investigations to determine whether the board should impose sanctions on those providers, such as revoking a provider's medical license.

CMS is not pursuing six practices that appear in two categories, prevention and detection and monitoring, because the agency considers the practices to be outside the scope of its program integrity activities, is concerned about limiting beneficiaries' access to services, or for other reasons.

- *Prevention, and Detection and Monitoring: Clinical Guidelines.* While CMS uses clinical guidelines to review plan sponsors' formularies to ensure access to certain drugs, CMS does not require plan sponsors to carry out activities within these program integrity practices, such as filling only the prescriptions for the lowest effective dose, promoting alternatives to opioids, or screening their patients for potential drug abuse. However, CMS provides training materials to providers on such topics to promote patient safety, and other parts of Medicare cover screening for drug abuse under certain conditions.
- *Prevention: Health Information Technology.* CMS does not use health information technology for program integrity purposes, but encourages its use by, for example, providing information to Medicare beneficiaries on the benefits of electronic health records.
- *Prevention: PDMPs.* CMS guidance to physicians has encouraged prescribers to check their states' PDMP prior to prescribing certain

drugs; however, variations in state practices regarding access to PDMPs means that not all prescribers may be able to conduct checks, according to CMS officials.

- *Prevention: Limit the Supply of Abused Drugs*. CMS officials told us that the agency does not conduct activities to limit the supply of abused drugs because this practice is beyond the scope of Part D program integrity efforts. For example, CMS does not operate "take back" days where beneficiaries can dispose of any unneeded prescription drugs, since, until recently, DEA required a law enforcement presence at such events, which CMS cannot provide.[26] CMS also does not address the supply of abuse-resistant drugs, officials said, since that is the responsibility of the Food and Drug Administration and pharmaceutical manufacturers.
- *Detection and Monitoring: Lock-ins*. CMS does not monitor Medicare beneficiaries through a "lock-in" or restricted recipient program. We previously recommended that CMS consider a restricted recipient program for Medicare Part D that would limit certain beneficiaries to one prescriber, one pharmacy, or both for receiving prescriptions, and that the agency should seek congressional authority, as appropriate, to do so. [27] CMS, in responding to our recommendation, stated that it did not agree that a restricted recipient program was necessarily the appropriate control for the Part D program, and raised concerns about restricting beneficiaries' access to services.[28] However, in August 2014, OIG recommended that CMS restrict certain beneficiaries to a limited number of pharmacies and prescribers, and CMS concurred with the recommendation, but stated the agency needs—and is receptive to—legislative authority to "lock in" beneficiaries in Part D.[29]

  Currently, the agency requires plan sponsors to review data to identify beneficiaries potentially at risk for overutilization of certain drugs, including opioids, and to monitor those beneficiaries.[30] Monitoring may include notifying their prescribers of the overutilization, case management, and point-of-sale edits, which are beneficiary-specific edits that can vary based on the situation. For example, the edits may prevent a beneficiary from receiving certain types of prescription drugs or an excessive amount of a particular drug.[31]

See appendix I for the status of all 23 program integrity practices we identified and whether CMS and its contractors have implemented, planned to implement, or are not pursuing them.

AGENCY COMMENTS

We provided a draft of this report to the Department of Health and Human Services (HHS) for comment and HHS provided written comments. In its comments, HHS generally agreed with our findings, and provided more information regarding our finding that CMS is not pursuing 6 of the 23 practices we identified for prescription drug fraud, waste, and abuse. Generally, the agency provided additional information for why CMS is not pursuing certain practices as part of its program integrity efforts, such as the use of clinical guidelines, PDMPs, and lock-in programs. Regarding the practice of health information technology, while HHS noted that CMS requires the development by Part D sponsors of electronic prescription drug programs and the use of e-prescribing is encouraged, these activities were not identified by CMS officials as specific program integrity efforts. Regarding the practice of limiting the supply of abused drugs, HHS described CMS activities that we considered under a different practice—the use of prepayment edits. Our descriptions and examples of these practices, as well as the other 17 practices, are included in tables 1, 2, and 3 in this report. HHS also provided a recent example of its program integrity efforts to address fraud, waste, and abuse in the Part D program, in which HHS sent letters to providers identified as very high prescribers of certain controlled substances to give information to these providers to help them evaluate whether their high prescribing level of these drugs is appropriate for their patient population, and to identify areas where their prescribing could be modified. HHS also provided technical comments, which we incorporated as appropriate.

Sincerely yours,
Kathleen King
Director, Health Care

Appendix I: Status of Practices by CMS and Its Contractors to Address Prescription Drug Fraud, Waste, and Abuse

Table 5 shows the 23 prevention, detection and monitoring, and investigation and prosecution practices we identified, their CMS status (implemented, planned, or not pursuing), and examples of the activities. We determined that CMS had implemented a practice if the agency required or documented at least one activity within that practice, that CMS planned a practice if documentation or officials described activities as pilots or in the process of development, and that CMS was not pursuing practices based on reviews of documentation and interviews with officials.

Table 5. CMS Implementation Status and Examples of 23 Prevention, Detection and Monitoring, and Investigation and Prosecution Practices GAO Identified

Category	Practice	Status ●Implemented ☼Planned ○Not pursuing	Responsible entities, examples of activities,[a] or explanation of status
Prevention	Clinical guidelines (prevention)	○	The Centers for Medicare & Medicaid Services (CMS) does not use clinical guidelines for program integrity purposes, but the agency provides educational materials related to appropriate prescribing.
	Collaboration (prevention)	●	CMS has established relationships with a variety of stakeholders to help develop programs and strategies to address prescription drug fraud, waste, and abuse, including, for example, the agency's participation in the Public-Private Partnership to Prevent Health Care Fraud and as a member of the National Health Care Anti-Fraud Association.
	Education (prevention)	●	Outreach & Education Medicare Drug Integrity Contractor (O&E MEDIC), in concert with CMS

Table 5. (Continued)

Category	Practice	Status ●Implemented ☼Planned ○Not pursuing	Responsible entities, examples of activities,[a] or explanation of status
			Center for Program Integrity, offers a variety of materials and events, such as an insert on safe drug disposal that plan sponsors can provide to their beneficiaries and training to Medicare beneficiaries on how to prevent potential fraud.
	Health information technology	○	CMS does not use health information technology for program integrity purposes, but has encouraged its use, such as by providing information to Medicare beneficiaries on the benefits of electronic health records.
	Limit the supply of abused drugs	○	CMS does not limit the supply of abused drugs because the associated activities of this practice are beyond the scope of Part D program integrity efforts, according to CMS officials. For example, until recently, to accept unneeded controlled substances in a "take back" program, the Drug Enforcement Administration required a law enforcement presence, which CMS cannot provide.
	Prepayment edits	●	Plan sponsors may implement edits at the point of sale to control specific beneficiaries' access to certain medications (see also drug utilization review (DUR) below). For every prescription, plan sponsors must check a range of information, typically at the point of sale or distribution, such as drug interactions, incorrect amounts, and age or gender contraindications, such as a woman receiving

Category	Practice	Status ●Implemented ☼Planned ○Not pursuing	Responsible entities, examples of activities,[a] or explanation of status
			medications prescribed only to men.
	Screening	●	Plan sponsors must verify beneficiaries' Part D eligibility. CMS finalized a rule in May 2014 establishing a Medicare enrollment requirement for Part D prescribers effective June 1, 2015, and strengthening screening for ineligible incarcerated beneficiaries starting January 1, 2015.[b]
	Prescription Drug Monitoring Programs (PDMP)c(Prevention)	○	CMS guidance encourages but does not require prescribers to check PDMPs prior to prescribing and variations in state practices mean not all prescribers may be able to conduct checks.
Detection and monitoring (D&M)	Clinical guidelines (D&M)	○	CMS does not use clinical guidelines for Part D program integrity purposes, but other parts of Medicare provide training materials to providers, such as on the topic of coverage for Screening, Brief Intervention, and Referral to Treatment services to identify, reduce, and prevent problematic substance use, abuse, and dependence.
	Collaboration (D&M)	●	Plan sponsors are to share information with CMS regarding potentially fraudulent providers or schemes. National Benefit Integrity (NBI) and O&E MEDICs convene conferences and share information on prescription drug fraud, waste, and abuse with plan sponsors, law enforcement, beneficiaries, and other stakeholders. CMS sends memos to all plan sponsors about new Part D fraud schemes and potentially fraudulent

Table 5. (Continued)

Category	Practice	Status ●Implemented ☼Planned ○Not pursuing	Responsible entities, examples of activities,[a] or explanation of status
			providers that are also made available on the O&E MEDIC website. In addition, CMS sends theresults of the NBI MEDIC's data analyses directly to a plan sponsor if the NBI MEDIC identifies particular issues for that sponsor to address.
	Compliance program	●	Plan sponsors are to have effective compliance programs.
	Data analysis	●	The NBI MEDIC conducts data analysis projects, such as identifying deceased prescribers across all plan sponsors, and is to have clinical and analytic staff to conduct that work. The NBI MEDIC is also implementing predictive analytic models to identify potential fraud in the Part D program. Plan sponsors are to have clinical and analytic staff, or contract with an entity that can provide such staff, to monitor and analyze data as part of their compliance programs.
	Drug utilization review (DUR)	●	Plan sponsors are to review beneficiaries' drug utilization patterns to identify potential patient harm and beneficiaries at risk for overutilization, and refer those beneficiaries for case management. Plan sponsors are to share information on these beneficiaries when they move from one Part D plan to another. CMS also reports quarterly to plan sponsors the names of their beneficiaries overutilizing opioids and certain other drugs through

Category	Practice	Status ●Implemented ☼Planned ○Not pursuing	Responsible entities, examples of activities,[a] or explanation of status
			CMS's Overutilization Monitoring System. Plan sponsors must report to CMS quarterly how each identified case is addressed.
	Education (D&M)	●	O&E MEDIC, in coordination with CMS and the NBI MEDIC, provides training and materials to plan sponsors and others on how to identify potential fraud, waste, and abuse. For example, the O&E MEDIC, with CMS oversight, developed a Fraud Handbook that plan sponsors can access to learn about practical techniques and approaches on preventing, detecting, and investigating potential prescription drug fraud.
	Recipient restriction programs ("lock-ins")	○	CMS does not monitor Medicare beneficiaries through a "lock-in" program. The agency has reported that it has taken a beneficiary-centric approach that discourages such restrictions, and lacks the legislative authority to implement such a program, although the agency has stated that it is receptive to such authority. In addition, in 2012, CMS conducted a study that identified few beneficiaries (less than 1 percent) who would merit such a program[d] (see also DUR above).
	PDMPs[c](D&M)	☼	CMS is negotiating with a national organization to obtain access to its PDMP data.
	Postpayment reviews	●	Plan sponsors are to conduct certain postpayment reviews (see also DUR above). Plan sponsors are also to provide beneficiaries with an explanation-of-benefits document to review for

Table 5. (Continued)

Category	Practice	Status ●Implemented ☼Planned ○Not pursuing	Responsible entities, examples of activities,[a] or explanation of status
			potential errors that also has a telephone number to report potential fraud. Part D Recovery Audit Contractor is to review paid Part D claims to identify over- and underpayments and recoup overpayments, and refer potential fraud identified during that postpayment review to the NBI MEDIC.
Investigation and prosecution (I&P)	Collaboration (I&P)	●	The NBI MEDIC responds to law enforcement requests for information and has participated in task forces and other investigative efforts. The O&E MEDIC trains insurance investigators, law enforcement and others. CMS hosts quarterly meetings with a variety of stakeholders on prescription drug fraud, waste, and abuse.
	Education (I&P)	●	The O&E MEDIC, in consultation with the NBI MEDIC, provides educational materials on how to investigate potential fraud.
	Enforcement	☼	Starting June 1, 2015, CMS may revoke prescribers' Medicare enrollment band CMS officials reported they are starting to work with the Health and Human Services Office of Inspector General (OIG) to remove more providers from Medicare through "permissive exclusions."[e]
	Investigations/ investigative staff	●	Plan sponsors are to have staff who can identify potential fraud. The NBI MEDIC is to have investigative staff knowledgeable of

Category	Practice	Status ●Implemented ☼Planned ○Not pursuing	Responsible entities, examples of activities,[a] or explanation of status
			prescription drug fraud.
	Reporting to law enforcement	●	The NBI MEDIC is required to refer investigations to law enforcement. CMS encourages but does not require plan sponsors to refer potential fraud to law enforcement and/or CMS, including the NBIMEDIC.[f]
	PDMPs[c] (I&P)	☼	CMS is negotiating with certain states to obtain access to their PDMP data.

Source: GAO analysis of CMS documents and interviews with officials. | GAO-15-66

[a] This table does not include all instances of CMS's activities to implement the practices we identified.

[b] Once prescribers are enrolled, the rule provides that CMS will be able to revoke prescriber billing privileges for certain abuses of the program or noncompliance with applicable licensure requirements. To implement the exclusion of incarcerated individuals from Part D coverage, the rule redefined eligible Medicare service areas to exclude facilities in which individuals are incarcerated. See Medicare Program: Contract Year 2015 Policy and Technical Changes to the Medicare Advantage and the Medicare Prescription Drug Benefit Programs. 79 Fed. Reg. 29,844 (May 23, 2014).

[c] PDMPs are state-based programs that operate electronic databases that gather information from pharmacies on certain dispensed prescriptions. Authorized users access the information about a patients' prescription drug history, such as whether a patient has multiple opioid prescriptions from multiple providers.

[d] In 2012, CMS analyzed Part D data to identify beneficiaries receiving potentially unsafe doses of prescription opioids for 90 or more consecutive days, excluding beneficiaries with cancer or in hospice care. CMS concluded that .71 percent (224,964) of all Part D beneficiaries were at high risk for potential adverse effects and had a high likelihood of inappropriately using opioids. CMS also analyzed the number of prescribers and pharmacies associated with these beneficiaries' opioid prescriptions and found that .07 percent (22,222) of Part D beneficiaries received high dosages of opioids from at least four prescribers and at least four pharmacies.

[e] Under section 1128 of the Social Security Act, exclusions from federal health programs are permissive under certain circumstances and mandatory in others. 42 U.S.C. § 1320a-7. Permissive exclusions are allowed for a variety of reasons, including licensure suspension, surrender, or revocation, or misdemeanor controlled substance conviction. Mandatory exclusions are required for felony

convictions relating to health care fraud or controlled substances and any convictions relating to patient abuse/neglect or to the delivery of Medicare or state health care programs.

[f] In a March 2014 report, OIG reiterated previous recommendations that it had made to CMS to amend regulations to require Part D plan sponsors to report to CMS their identification of and response to potential fraud and abuse incidents. CMS did not concur with this recommendation, citing concerns about creating duplicative reporting. See Department of Health and Human Services Office of Inspector General, Less than Half of Part D Sponsors Voluntarily Reported Data on Potential Fraud and Abuse, OEI-03-13-00030 (Washington, D.C.: March 2014). CMS officials told us in September 2014 that if the agency were to impose such a requirement, it would be able to evaluate sponsors' compliance with the reporting requirement, but not whether the reports identified actual fraud as defined by law enforcement.

End Notes

[1] Fraud involves an intentional act or representation to deceive with the knowledge that the action or representation could result in gain. Waste includes inaccurate payments for services, such as unintentional duplicate payments. Abuse represents actions inconsistent with acceptable business or medical practices. In this report, we use the term "program integrity" to refer to activities and practices that address fraud, waste, and abuse.

[2] Medicare is a federal health insurance program for people age 65 and older, individuals under age 65 with certain disabilities, and individuals diagnosed with end-stage renal disease. Medicare Parts A and B are known as original Medicare or Medicare fee-for-service; Part A covers hospital and other inpatient stays, and Part B covers hospital outpatient, physician, and other services. Part C is Medicare Advantage, under which beneficiaries receive health benefits through private health plans. In Part D, plan sponsors offer prescription drug coverage through stand-alone prescription drug plans or through Medicare Advantage prescription drug plans, which combine medical and prescription drug benefits.

In 1990, we began to report on government operations that we identified as "high risk" for serious weaknesses in areas that involve substantial resources and provide critical services to the public. Medicare has been included among such programs since 1990. See GAO, High-Risk Series: An Update, GAO-13-283 (Washington, D.C.: Feb. 14, 2013).

[3] See, for example, Department of Health and Human Services Office of Inspector General, Prescribers with Questionable Patterns in Medicare Part D, OEI-02-09-00603 (Washington, D.C.: June 2013); MEDIC Benefit Integrity Activities in Medicare Parts C and D, OEI-03-11-00310 (Washington, D.C.: January 2013); and GAO, Medicare Part D: Instances of Questionable Access to Prescription Drugs, GAO-11-699 (Washington, D.C.: Sept. 6, 2011).

[4] We interviewed a total of 14 stakeholder groups: the National Health Care Anti-Fraud Association and the Health Care Compliance Association, which represent antifraud and compliance entities; AARP, which represents Medicare beneficiaries; America's Health Insurance Plans, which represents private insurers; the Academy of Managed Care

Pharmacy, the American Pharmacists Association, the National Association of Chain Drug Stores, and the National Community Pharmacists Association, which represent pharmacies; the Pharmaceutical Care Management Association, which represents pharmacy benefit managers; the American Medical Association, which represents prescribers; and the Federation of State Medical Boards, the National Association of Attorneys General, the National Association of Medicaid Fraud Control Units, the National Association of Medicaid Directors, and the Prescription Drug Monitoring Programs Center for Excellence, which represent state-based programs.

[5] The Fraud Prevention Framework was developed by GAO and informed by GAO's internal control standards for the federal government. See GAO, Individual Disaster Assistance Programs: Framework for Fraud Prevention, Detection, and Prosecution, GAO-06-954T (Washington, D.C.: July 12, 2006). We are currently considering revisions to the Fraud Prevention Framework, which we plan to publish in 2015.

[6] In this report, we use the term "plan sponsors" to refer to both stand-alone Part D plan sponsors as well as Medicare Advantage prescription drug sponsors.

[7] To protect beneficiaries and the fiscal integrity of the Medicare program, the Medicare Prescription Drug, Improvement, and Modernization Act of 2003 (MMA), which established the Part D program, requires all Part D sponsors to have programs to safeguard Part D from fraud, waste, and abuse. Pub. L. No. 108-173 § 101, 117 Stat. 2066, 2086 (codified at 42 U.S.C. § 1395w-104(c)(1)(D)). As a result, CMS issued regulations requiring that sponsors adopt and implement a compliance program that includes measures to prevent, detect, and correct fraud, waste, and abuse. 42 C.F.R. § 423.504(b)(4)(vi).

[8] CMS Compliance Program Guidelines appear in Chapter 9 of the Medicare Prescription Drug Benefit Manual, revised January 11, 2013. CMS issues this manual in tandem with Chapter 21 of the Medicare Managed Care Manual, which includes the Compliance Program Guidelines for Medicare Advantage.

[9] Beginning in fiscal year 2007, CMS awarded contracts to MEDICs to address potential fraud and abuse related to the Part D benefit. In fiscal year 2009, CMS added oversight of Part C to the MEDICs' responsibilities.

[10] Every time a Medicare beneficiary fills a prescription covered under Part D, the sponsor must submit a prescription drug event record to CMS. These records include drug cost and payment information that enables CMS to administer and monitor the Part D benefit.

[11] Among other things, the Controlled Substances Act requires those who manufacture, distribute, prescribe, import, or export controlled substances to register with the DEA. 21 U.S.C. §§ 822, 957. Once registered, DEA provides a certificate with a registration number.

[12] CMS evaluates each MEDIC's performance annually based on metrics it sets for each contractor, primarily related to the timeliness of contractors' work. For example, CMS expects that the NBI MEDIC will send an acknowledgment letter to complainants within 5 days of receiving the complaint, and expects that the O&E MEDIC will conduct a minimum of 10 training presentations each contract year. Scores are based on a five-point scale: (1) unsatisfactory, (2) marginal, (3) satisfactory, (4) very good, and (5) exceptional.

CMS rated the contractors on additional elements not included in the examples we described.

[13] The NBI MEDIC's most recently completed Contractor Performance Assessment Reports System (CPARS) evaluation was for April 2011 through March 2012. While CMS has conducted two subsequent reviews, the ratings had not been posted to CPARS as of August 2014. Therefore, we report the MEDIC's 2013 activities from the most recently completed

contract year, and the CPARS ratings as of March 2012, since those are the most recently available results.

[14] The O&E MEDIC's most recently completed contract year for which its CPARS ratings are available was October 2012 through September 2013

[15] PDMPs are state-based programs that operate electronic databases that gather information from pharmacies on certain dispensed prescriptions, such as whether a patient has multiple opioid prescriptions from multiple providers. Authorized users access the information about a patient's prescription drug history. Each state determines what data are collected, and who may access the PDMP and for what purpose. For example, some states only allow health care providers to access the PDMP as a patient-safety tool for their patients, while others allow law enforcement access for active investigations. According to Brandeis University's PDMP Training and Technical Assistance Center, as of June 2014, 49 of 50 states and the District of Columbia had legislation authorizing PDMPs, and 48 of those have operational PDMPs.

[16] Medicare Program: Contract Year 2015 Policy and Technical Changes to the Medicare Advantage and the Medicare Prescription Drug Benefit Programs. 79 Fed. Reg. 29,844 (May 23, 2014).

[17] Under section 1128 of the Social Security Act, exclusions from federal health programs are permissive under certain circumstances and mandatory in others. 42 U.S.C. § 1320a7. Permissive exclusions are allowed for a variety of reasons, including licensure suspension, surrender, or revocation, or misdemeanor controlled substance conviction. Mandatory exclusions are required for felony convictions relating to health care fraud or controlled substances, and any convictions relating to patient abuse/neglect or to the delivery of Medicare or state health care programs.

[18] Medicare Program: Contract Year 2015 Policy and Technical Changes to the Medicare Advantage and the Medicare Prescription Drug Benefit Programs. 79 Fed. Reg. 29,844 (May 23, 2014).

[19] Id.

[20] See Department of Health and Human Services Office of Inspector General, Medicare Improperly Paid Millions of Dollars for Prescription Drugs Provided to Incarcerated Beneficiaries during 2006 through 2010, A-07-12-06035 (Washington, D.C.: January 2014); and The Centers for Medicare & Medicaid Services Provided Medicare Part D Coverage to Beneficiaries Confined in Mental Health Facilities for Court-Ordered Purposes, A-07-13-06041 (Washington, D.C.: July 2014).

[21] PLATO stands for "predictive learning analytics tracking outcome." Predictive analytic technologies are a variety of automated systems and tools that can be used to identify particular types of behavior, including fraud, before transactions are completed.

[22] CMS selects sponsors to audit based on size, past audit findings, and risk, selecting both sponsors that may serve as role models, as well as those that are at risk. As of August 2014, CMS officials reported that 97 percent of beneficiaries are enrolled with plan sponsors that have been audited. CMS's 2013 audit findings included a lack of evidence that plan sponsors' FDRs or governing bodies were trained in compliance or in how to identify and report potential fraud, waste, or abuse; a lack of evidence that plan sponsors were conducting reasonable inquiries of potential fraud, waste, or abuse in a timely manner; and a lack of evidence that plan sponsors were implementing procedures to ensure appropriate corrective actions were taken in response to potential fraud, waste, or abuse.

[23] Corrective action plans are developed by the plan sponsor to address deficiencies identified by CMS. Plans are to provide an attainable time frame for implementing corrective actions,

and include a process for validating and monitoring that the corrective actions were taken and remain effective.

A CMS official noted that stricter penalties—specifically, civil money penalties—are reserved for weaknesses that result in direct adverse effects on beneficiaries, such as not being able to access medications and care.

[24] Medicare Program: Contract Year 2015 Policy and Technical Changes to the Medicare Advantage and the Medicare Prescription Drug Benefit Programs. 79 Fed. Reg. 1,918 (proposed Jan. 10, 2014).

[25] Both GAO and OIG have reported problems with CMS's audits of Part D plan sponsors. See GAO, Medicare Part D: Some Plan Sponsors Have Not Completely Implemented Fraud and Abuse Programs, and CMS Oversight Has Been Limited, GAO-08-760 (Washington, D.C.: July 21, 2008), and Department of Health and Human Services Office of Inspector General, Audits of Medicare Prescription Drug Plan Sponsors, OEI-03-09- 00330 (Washington, D.C.: December 2011).

[26] DEA finalized a rule effective October 9, 2014, expanding the options available to dispose of controlled substances. See Disposal of Controlled Substances. 79 Fed. Reg. 53,520 (Sept. 9, 2014).

[27] See GAO-11-699. In that report, CMS policy officials stated that Part D cannot have a restricted recipient program because MMA, which established the Part D program, did not authorize CMS to establish such restrictions on beneficiaries.

[28] Following our report, in 2012 CMS conducted a study that identified few beneficiaries (less than 1 percent) who would merit a lock-in program. CMS analyzed Part D data to identify beneficiaries receiving potentially unsafe doses of prescription opioids for 90 or more consecutive days, excluding beneficiaries with cancer or in hospice care. CMS concluded that .71 percent (224,964) of all Part D beneficiaries were at high risk for potential adverse effects and had a high likelihood of inappropriately using opioids. CMS also analyzed the number of prescribers and pharmacies associated with these beneficiaries' opioid prescriptions and found that .07 percent (22,222) of Part D beneficiaries received high dosages of opioids from at least four prescribers and at least four pharmacies.

[29] See Department of Health and Human Services Office of Inspector General, Part D Beneficiaries with Questionable Utilization Patterns for HIV Drugs, OEI-02-11-00170 (Washington, D.C.: August 2014).

[30] CMS requires plan sponsors to have drug utilization review (DUR) programs that include retrospective reviews of claims and case management for drugs susceptible to abuse, including opioids. 42 C.F.R § 423.153. Starting in 2013, CMS implemented a Medicare Part D Overutilization Monitoring System (OMS). OMS is similar and in addition to the DUR programs, but is focused on opioids and certain other drugs, and includes CMS sending quarterly reports to plan sponsors to alert them to their beneficiaries who are receiving excessive amounts of those drugs.

OIG recommended in August 2014 that CMS expand both the plan sponsors' DUR programs and OMS to include additional drugs susceptible to fraud, waste, and abuse. CMS concurred with the recommendation to expand DUR programs, noting the agency already encourages plan sponsors to examine nonopioids as part of those programs. CMS did not concur that it should similarly expand OMS, stating that the program is a "safety-focused tool," not a "fraud identification tool." See OEI-02-11-00170.

[31] Beneficiaries have a right to appeal the use of these edits, as set forth at 42 C.F.R. Part 423, Subpart M, and Chapter 18 of the Medicare Prescription Drug Benefit Manual.

INDEX

G

H

I

L

M

N

O

P

U

V

W